The Solo Girl's Guide to Becoming a Digital Nomad

Claire Summers

© Copyright 2019 Claire Summers - All rights reserved.

The content contained within this book may not be reproduced, duplicated or transmitted without direct written permission from the author or the publisher.

Under no circumstances will any blame or legal responsibility be held against the publisher, or author, for any damages, reparation, or monetary loss due to the information contained within this book. Either directly or indirectly.

Legal Notice:

This book is copyright protected. This book is only for personal use. You cannot amend, distribute, sell, use, quote or paraphrase any part, or the content within this book, without the consent of the author or publisher.

Disclaimer Notice:

Please note the information contained within this document is for educational and entertainment purposes only. All effort has been executed to present accurate, up to date, and reliable, complete information. No warranties of any kind are declared or implied. Readers acknowledge that the author is not engaging in the rendering of legal, financial, medical, or professional advice. The content within this book has been derived from various sources. Please consult a licensed professional before attempting any techniques outlined in this book.

By reading this document, the reader agrees that under no circumstances is the author responsible for any losses, direct or indirect, which are incurred as a result of the use of information contained within this document, including, but not limited to, errors, omissions, or inaccuracies.

This book would not have been possible without the wonderful people who have supported me on this journey. So, I dedicate this book to my family, friends, and all the travel companions I've met along the way.

Table of Contents

Forward 7
Chapter 1 - A bit about me 8
Chapter 2 - The Starting Point 13
    Stage 1 - Peace 14
    Stage 2 - Doubt 15
    Stage 3 - Excitement 16
    Stage 4 - Focus 17
    Stage 5 - What the FUCK did I do? 18
    Stage 6 - Freedom 19
Chapter 3 - Getting Prepared 21
    Mentally 21
    Physically 23
    Preparing your family 24
    Tips for dealing with over-anxious friends and family: 29
    Solo Traveling Over 30 30
Chapter 4 - Money 33
    Saving money vs. paying off your debts 34
    My top money-saving tips 35
Chapter 5 - Finding a Digital Nomad Job 39
    What kind of location-independent professional will you be? 39
    How easy is it to become a digital nomad? 41
    Digital Nomad Courses 43
    Digital Nomad Job/Gig Hunting 47
    Digital Nomad Resources 47
Chapter 6 - Show Me The Money 50
Chapter 7 - Planning 53
    4 Questions to Determine Where You're Headed 56
    More Questions to Answer Before You Leave 58
Chapter 8 - Packing 64
    My Packing Philosophy 64
    Packing Logistics 66
    What to Pack 66

Chapter 9 - Traveling Solo ... 74
    What Kind of Traveler Are You? ... 75

Chapter 10 - Safety ... 78
    Research: Because Knowledge Is Power ... 79
    Emergency Numbers ... 80
    Booking Your Accommodations ... 80
    Public Transportation Safety Tips ... 81
    Using Google Maps for Safety ... 82
    Pin Dropping ... 83
    Safety Items ... 83
    Important Documents ... 84
    Money and Credit Cards ... 84
    Utilizing Facebook Groups for Safety ... 85
    Watch Your Drinks ... 86
    Insurance ... 87
    Trust Your Intuition ... 88

Chapter 11 - Dealing with Fear ... 89

Chapter 12 - Finding Your Community ... 94
    Where can you find your community? ... 94
    Dealing with all the Goodbyes ... 96
    Networking ... 97
    Overcoming Loneliness ... 97

Chapter 13 - Working On The Road ... 100
    Time Management ... 100
    Where to Work ... 101

Chapter 14 - Volunteering ... 103

Chapter 15 - Logistics ... 106
    Go Paperless ... 108
    Using a postal service ... 109

Chapter 16 – Technology ... 110
    What Technology Will You Need as a DN? ... 111
    Digital Nomad-Friendly Software, Cloud Storage, and Apps ... 112

Chapter 18 - It's Okay To Go Home ... 115

Chapter 17 - When Things Go Wrong ... 116
    The Scorpion Incident ... 116
    Broke and Robbed in Bogota ... 117

Chapter 19 - Conclusion ... 121

About the Author 122

Acknowledgments

I wanted to write this book for the longest time but I just never seemed to find the time to sit and write, so I need to give a special thank you to Dana Kantrowitz my editor. If it wasn't for her prodding me for more chapters and setting my deadlines this book would likely still be a jumble of ideas in my head.

To Pamela Dobson, thank you for your edits and incredible generosity in sharing your knowledge of self-publishing with me to help me navigate this new world.

To everyone who has read my blog and supported my journey so far, it's been a crazy few years and I look forward too many more.

And finally, I must acknowledge my mother, Janice. Although we often drive each other crazy, less so these past years. Her strength and determination continue to inspire me more than words can ever express. In the same week I have been putting the finishing touches on this book, she has been doing the same to her PhD dissertation. We both left school at 16 so, our individual journeys through education with the written word have not always been straight forward or simple. Maybe one day I will follow in her footsteps and return to academia to compete a PhD of my own.

Forward

Search for #digitalnomad and you'll be swamped with images of MacBooks, lattes, and beach views. You'll find everything from blog posts to *New York Times* articles about these global wanderers who binge on travel experiences while hustling from their laptops. The Digital Nomad lifestyle—that is, being able to work from anywhere in the world with decent Wi-Fi—is the dream, isn't it?

Well, yes, but it does have its challenges and downsides. Being a remote worker, location independent, full-time traveler, nomadic wanderer, or whatever you call it, can be emotionally, mentally, and physically draining. It's not the right lifestyle just because you love to travel.

Being a digital nomad is not a permanent vacation. But it remains the best choice I've ever made for myself.

Are you thinking of leaving behind a more traditional lifestyle to travel while working? Curious how I did this and came out alive (and happier and healthier) on the other side? Well, I don't have a universal how-to manual that's guaranteed to get you from your current job, home, and personal commitments to a no-strings-attached, location-independent lifestyle. But, I'll share with you how I came to the decision to become nomadic, what steps I took, and what I learned along the way that you can apply to your own situation.

Fair Warning: I spent five years in the British Navy, so I literally have a mouth like a sailor. And I'm dead honest. I may overshare a bit while dishing on everything I wish I had known before I flew far

far away from what I thought was my life in exchange for an adventure as a digital nomad.

Chapter 1 - A bit about me

I'm Claire, and I'm a serial over-packer. It's a personality trait you'd assume that being an experienced traveler would correct, but I've been a digital nomad for 3 years, 1 month and 24 days, and yet here we are.

The most difficult question I get asked is, "what do you do for a living?" My answer depends on the day of the week and where I am in the world.

While you may assume that being a digital nomad means you're a techie, I'm living proof that you can earn an income in many different industries and with a variety of skillsets while seeing the world. Here are some of the jobs I have done (and some I still do) in chronological order:

Newspaper deliverer
Waitress
Farm worker
Bar staff
Hair salon receptionist
Coffee shop manager
Supermarket store legal and stock loss manager
Royal Navy logistics core
Makeup artist
Community dance practitioner
Professional dancer, choreographer, and dance producer
Massage therapist
Reiki practitioner

Artistic Director of a dance company
Fundraiser
Social media manager
Blogger
ESL teacher
Copywriter
Yoga teacher
SEO Wiz
Front end web developer
Co-director of a Digital Marketing Agency
Book author

It's a pretty eclectic list because I love to learn new skills, try novel things, and keep life moving. All of these jobs have helped make it possible for me to survive as a full-time traveler.

I wish I could tell you that my first year on the road was smooth sailing. But I'm not going to use a pretty filter to present a more flattering picture of reality. Eventually, I figured out how to travel while earning a livable salary. But the path was not always plain sailing. The lifestyle has forced me to draw on all of my skills, be creative, and take a lot of risks.

If you had asked me 10 years ago who I am and what I do, I would've told you I'm a dancer.

Most of my early life was spent in a dance studio. I left school at age 16 to train full time as a professional dancer. I dreamt of traveling the world as a dancer on cruise ships or in holiday parks. (Oh, the glam!) But that dream was quashed when I was injured at the end of my first year of professional dance training.

To have both my professional goals and travel aspirations ripped away from me was a huge blow. I identified as a dancer but could no longer consider dancing my future. I moved out of my family home and spent the next few years getting drunk, sinking into debt, and going slightly out of my mind on drugs.

By age 19, I was trying to drown my desire to travel. I didn't have the money. I had a crappy job in a supermarket working unsocial hours, a crappy boyfriend, and crappy career prospects thanks to my lack of education.

Because I had dropped out of school with no real qualifications, I couldn't go to university without preparatory classes, which I couldn't afford. So that was that. I felt stuck in my crappy life.

I was 21 when I hit rock bottom. I was on antidepressants, barely ate, and suffered crippling panic attacks. I knew if I kept moving in that direction, I was going to die. So I decided to sort out my shit. Make a big change. Shift the course of my life. Three months later, I was on an express train to the other side of the UK to undertake two months of military training.

The Royal Navy Rating who passed Phase 1 military training was not the same girl who boarded a train—frightened and full of hope—only weeks before.

My time with the Royal Navy, which went from an eight-week commitment to a five year career, was transformative. I visited new parts of the world, made new kinds of friends, and got to know new parts of myself. Not the dancer, not the drunk party girl, but the person who is capable of more than she realized. And *this* girl? She loves to travel.

The Navy paid me to see the world while advancing my education. When I left the Royal Navy, I had visited 16 countries, was on my way toward completing a teaching degree, and had updated my training as a makeup artist. The Navy paid for part of my university tuition so I could study dance. I'm so grateful to the military for the opportunities they offer and to that party girl for having the guts to make a life-changing decision.

With a new start, I decided to rededicate myself to my first love, the one that got away: dance.

I established a dance company called Exim Dance and served as Artistic Director. In the eight years following the completion of my university degree, I used dance as a means to visit places like Ghana, Vienna, and Seattle in the U.S. And I spent free time seeing Europe. But even with frequent holidays, I heard the siren call of travel and adventure growing louder and louder.

From the outside, I had everything I wanted, everything I had worked toward. For five years, I was the Artistic Director of a successful dance company. I toured as a professional dancer. As a dance producer, I was working on national, high profile projects. I was working with some seriously talented and supportive people.

But I felt trapped. First, the migraines started, then my old panic attacks returned. Before I knew it, I was on beta blockers and antidepressants. I couldn't sleep for months and couldn't drive thanks to my severe migraines.

When you seemingly have it all, it's hard to admit you're unhappy.

I let myself get swept up in a doomed relationship. My boyfriend was harmless, but let's be honest. He was pretty dumb but looked a bit like Gerard Butler in the movie *300*. I was being shallow AF. But, this guy was my way out.

He wanted to move back to his hometown (also known as one of the least attractive places to live in the UK, in the shadow of a nuclear power plant). I wanted a ticket out of my own life. I wanted out so badly that I agreed — one night after drunk sex — to move with him. I quit my job, told our roommates I was moving, and began making plans to take part of the dance company with me.

Boom. New life SORTED. I got to move somewhere that didn't really interest me, which is almost the same thing as traveling the world, right? Of course it's not. Maybe you can relate to this feeling: you're so unhappy with your current situation that you're willing to dive headfirst into a new one that you don't even want.

Luckily for me, the boyfriend cheated on me. Yes, this was actually a moment of good fortune for me because it suddenly changed my life. I halted my plans to move away with him and just fell apart. I told my office I was taking a week off and hopped on a train to the one place I felt safe and loved: home to Liverpool.

I needed to do some soul searching. I admitted to myself that I was never really into that guy, and I had allowed myself to commit to living a life I didn't want in a place I didn't want to live — all so I could escape. I was grieving the loss of the new start I had envisioned for myself. But I wasn't going to sit back and let that be the end to my story.

I didn't have a destination in mind. I didn't have a plan to get there. But I knew I needed to leave again and again and again. I'm Claire, and I'm a travel addict. You're still reading, so I bet you are, too.

Chapter 2 - The Starting Point

Admitting you want to leave is easy. Making the decision to leave, now that's the hard part.

Chances are you've spent most of your adult life working toward stability:
- secured a job
- found a nice place to live
- committed to a romantic partner

Maybe you went as far as buying a house, getting a dog, and filling your home with stuff you like. Maybe you settled down even more by starting a family. You leased a bigger car. Signed up for a gym membership. They recognize you at your neighborhood coffee shop.

You are settled right the fuck down.

When I decided to up and leave my life behind, I didn't own real estate, I didn't have a boyfriend, and still don't have any kids. But for so many of us, that is #goals, right? That's probably what your parents did, it's what most of your friends are aiming for, and it's probably what you thought you wanted — until you didn't.

When you realize you don't want a traditional lifestyle, and want to try life on the road, it can make your little world spin.

If you've come to this conclusion, there are a few things you may be feeling/thinking right now.

Shit.
Can someone make this stop? I want to get off now.
How did I let things get this far?

How the hell am I going to get out of my commitments?
I've worked so hard. I can't just give it all up and start over.
What if I give everything up then change my mind?
My mum is going to kill me.
I don't want to disappoint people.
There is no way I can just walk out on my life right now.
Maybe if I just keep buying nice things I'll forget I don't want to live like this anymore.
Fuck.

At this point in my own thinking, I was having a full-blown existential crisis. For three months, I questioned myself and challenged every excuse to maintain the status quo before I actually made the decision to leave and committed to becoming a digital nomad.

That period of debating and rationalizing includes what I call the 6 Stages of FML.

Stage 1 - Peace

When you realize you want to walk out on your life, you are likely to feel euphoric. It's a magical moment when your mind goes calm with epiphany.

For me, this stage is when I told myself *I know what I must do*. I have got to travel the world and be free.

Make the most of this feeling of peace and relish the confidence it can offer you because, trust me, this feeling of certainty isn't going to last long. Hold on to your pantyhose because chaos is coming.

Stage 2 - Doubt

This is the toughest stage. You are going to doubt yourself. You are going to second guess all of your choices and instincts and desires. And, unless you're lucky (as I was, thankfully), many of the people closest to you are going to fuel this self-doubt.

I can't do this.
I have responsibilities here.
I'll never be able to save enough money to travel.
What if I hate life on the road?
I don't think I'm capable of solo travel. Is it even safe?
What if I want to come back home when I no longer have one?
Is it too big a risk to give up everything I've worked so hard for?
My family thinks I'm being irresponsible.
My friends think I'm being selfish.
How will I pay my bills?
Why am I dissatisfied with a "normal" life?
Is this the right decision?
Am I really going to do this?

Let me answer your questions: YOU FUCKING GOT THIS!

What it comes down to is a really simple yes/no question: Do you want to go?

If your answer is 'no,' please put down this book and go read *Women Who Run with the Wolves* instead. In fact, even if you said 'yes,' you should read that book if you have a vagina.

If you answered 'yes,' I beg you to refer back to this statement every time you feel self-doubt creeping back in. Or shoot me an email and I'll remind you that YOU FUCKING GOT THIS.

I'm going to let you in on a little secret. Your life will never feel ready for you to become a full-time traveler. You will probably never have enough money to get up and go whenever, wherever you want. You will never know if you are independent enough or gutsy enough to pull this off unless you actually do it.

And here's another truth bomb. You can always come back to the community where you live now or move someplace else. There is no shame in trying something then deciding it's not right for you. I have more respect for someone who follows their dreams and learns that the grass wasn't actually greener on the other side than someone who wishes their life away playing it safe.

Stage 3 - Excitement

OMFG this is actually happening.

This is the fun stage. Make the most of this excitement because you're going to have moments over the coming days, weeks, and months when you're flooded with doubt again.

It's important to remember that excitement and anxiety are very similar reactions, both physically and emotionally. So, when you start to feel sick to your stomach with nervous energy and your mind is jumping from one possibility to another, just remember you feel like this when you're excited, too. In these moments, remind yourself, "I'm not nervous because I'm making the wrong decision. I'm excited because change feels scary and exhilarating, even when it's the right choice."

I know it sounds crazy. But, acknowledging this brain-body connection can help you manage the unavoidable feelings of anxiety and excitement you'll encounter throughout this life-changing decision you're making. Just take a few deep breaths and thank your body for letting you know you're alive and excited about life.

During this stage, I highly recommend you surround yourself with people who are supportive of your plans. It's going to greatly influence how you think and feel about your decision to become nomadic.

This is the time to start building your tribe.

Stage 4 - Focus

Otherwise known as plan and execute. This is when you're going to get shit done. Your to-do list at this stage should look something like this:

Save money
Sell all your crap
Buy new crap for new nomadic life
Sign up for a million and one online courses to train for remote work
Spend hours planning new life on Pinterest
Frantically try to tie up loose ends of your old life
Join every nomadic/solo travel/remote worker/backpacking group on Facebook
Find a private place to cry and contemplate your sanity
Start a blog (because if you don't publicly document your highs and lows, did they even happen?)

One thing you can already check off your list is acquiring this book. I'm going to cover all of these tasks (and tribulations and triumphs) in detail so you're prepared and pumped for the adventure ahead!

Refine your to-do list with achievable tasks with deadlines, so every item on your list is necessary and within your reach. Take a task like "learn how to work remotely" and turn it into "Register by February 10 for photo editing course with XYZ that begins on March 1."

Your plan will keep you grounded and save you from some of the head-spin you're likely to experience.

Stage 5 - What the FUCK did I do?

At some point, the magnitude of what you are about to do is going to hit you. For me, it happened a few weeks before I left.

I had just closed the door to my flat after a couple came and bought my crockery and duvet. I made a bed on my couch with my sleeping bag and settled down to watch a movie on my laptop. I looked around at my empty flat and burst into tears.

IT WAS ALL GONE.

Whatever didn't fit into the three small boxes I would store with a friend was sold. All of those nice things I worked so hard for - GONE. All of my homey comforts, like my favorite duvet and things not made of plastic to eat from - GONE. It looked like I had discarded my entire life. Yes, they were just things. But each thing had a story. My flat held so many memories. That my home was no longer mine rocked me to the core. At that moment, all I could think was: What the FUCK did I do?

So, what did I do? How does one deal with a meltdown of this magnitude?

I drank wine from a plastic cup, smoked a cigarette out of my window, and let myself feel all the feels. *You fucking got this*, I reminded myself, even though it felt like a lie at the time.

You're going to go through these moments, too. It's part of the process. It is difficult and messy and there may or may not be some ugly crying involved. But if you know this is the right decision for you, then you have to follow your intuition and let yourself feel all the good and bad that comes with it.

And remember, when it feels like too much, you can always whine with a good friend. I mean, wine. Wine is your friend.

Stage 6 - Freedom

Once you enter this stage, chances are, you'll spend the next few months flitting between stages 5 and 6 with a bit of stage 2 thrown in every now and then. Every time something is difficult in a new way, you will doubt yourself. But you'll get through it.

When I touched down in Guatemala (the first country I traveled to), I cried. But this was not a life-questioning breakdown. It felt like all of the emotion and pain I'd been carrying around was leaving my body. Or, as I like to call it, feelings-quietly-leaking-out-of-my-eyes crying. It was therapeutic.

I was suddenly telling myself a new story: I did it.

And you can, too. Fly high, my little bird. Fly far, far away!

Chapter 3 - Getting Prepared

If you have made it this far and still think that transitioning to the nomad life is the right choice for you, then it's time to get prepared. This chapter is all about planning and preparing yourself mentally and physically for what comes next.

Mentally

The biggest challenges you're likely to face when preparing to leave and living on the road are mental ones. From self-doubt to loneliness, you are going to feel it all. The best way to deal with it is to be prepared.

Ask yourself these questions: What makes me feel at peace? What keeps my feet on the ground when my mind is running in circles? What can I do for myself that makes me feel good, without being self-destructive?

For me, it's yoga and meditation. No matter how crazy things become, I get on my mat and take some time out to simply focus on my breath. It gives me a chance to reset, which has saved me many times over the years.

But yoga and meditation may not float your boat. So, what does? Journaling, running, playing sports, reading, cooking, playing an instrument, kickboxing, making art, singing, taking pictures, or walking through a park? Find the thing that works for you and do it every time you feel yourself distracted by negative emotions. I recommend doing this thing regularly to help prevent and lessen the intensity of anxious feelings. If you want to not only live the nomad lifestyle but succeed at it and feel fulfilled by it, you need to prioritize your mental wellbeing.

Have a crisis plan.

I know this may sound dramatic, but trust me, it's important to have a plan of action you can carry out if/when you feel your mental health taking a knock.

In my journal, I wrote my crisis plan on the back page so it's always easy to put my hands on. It looks something like this:

Make a cup of tea (so very British of me, I know).
Meditate for 10 minutes.
Find a yoga class.
Write down five things I'm thankful for.
Message a friend and tell them I'm having a down day.
Call my mum.
Go dancing.
Eat ice cream.

In those moments when you're exhausted from travel, missing your home and the normality of your old life, and just want to stay in bed and binge-watch [insert favorite TV show] all day, refer to your crisis plan. Staying in bed isn't going to make you feel better about yourself nor your situation. But moving through your crisis plan will.

Or, binge-watch Grey's Anatomy then work through your list the next day. Sometimes it's ok to wallow. I often allow myself to do this when I've been traveling too much and I'm overtired.

The idea is to get this plan in place now so you can rely on it throughout every stage of this process. Preparing mentally is just as important as deciding which clothes to pack. In fact, no, it's more important. You can buy new clothes. You can't replace your health.

Physically

Have you ever carried 15-20 kg on your back with sunburned shoulders in 90-degree heat while trying to navigate your way around a new town? I have and it is miserable.

Whether you're backpacking or pulling around a roller suitcase, you're going to have to lift and carry it at some point—and probably up and down stairs. I think you should be able to carry (without someone else's assistance) everything you're taking with you on the road. There will definitely be times when you have to walk from your Airbnb/hostel/hotel to a subway or train platform (stairs) or onto a bus (steps) or from the bus stop or metro station to your destination (think cobblestone streets and dirt roads) without the assistance of an Uber or taxi driver.

Now imagine that you're rushing so you won't miss your train, bus, metro, or flight. You aren't familiar with the area or don't know exactly where to go, so you're looking at the map on your phone while lugging around everything you own.

It's worth trying to prepare for scenarios like this, not only by packing as light as you can, but by getting physically stronger before you leave home. Adopt a fitness routine you can commit to because a life of travel will take its toll on your body. All that Pad Thai washed down with beer will catch up with you. Spending hours sitting on a bus is hard on the back. And, an erratic sleep schedule in uncomfortable beds can wear you out.

I recommend finding a home workout or some type of exercise you can enjoy without having to find (and pay for) a gym or studio everywhere you go. This could be yoga (YouTube routines and tutorials are great), jogging around the neighborhood or a nearby park, or a fitness program you can do at home without equipment.

Get into a solid routine at least a couple months before you hit the road. Regular exercise will help you manage the emotional stress of preparing to enter the nomad life while prepping your body for the physical challenges ahead. Maintaining your fitness routine while you travel will help you feel accomplished and ready to explore new places.

In your traditional life at home, you may not be very active. But, as a traveler, you'll find yourself with more opportunities for city walking, countryside biking, jungle trekking, mountain hiking, kayaking, surfing, rock climbing, or skiing. Being in shape will make these activities more accessible and enjoyable.

Preparing your family

Telling your friends and family that you're leaving the city or country may be the hardest part of this process. Convincing them that this is the best decision for you is probably impossible.

My situation was unique, as my mum and sister both already lived overseas, my brother drives bands around Europe for a living, and for most of my adult life, I lived a six-hour drive away. My family was fully aware of my restless nature and desire to travel. So, when I announced that I was selling all of my shit and going to Guatemala for who knows how long, no one was shocked. They did, however, have a lot of concerns and questions, which sounded like this:

Why can't you just be happy where you are?

Why Guatemala? It's so far away!

Is Guatemala even safe?

What if you get kidnapped?

What will you do for money?

Do you even speak Spanish?

How are you ever going to find a husband if you're traveling all the time?

Don't you want children?

Why can't you just take a sabbatical or vacation?

Is it really a good idea to travel on your own?

Over the months that passed while I was preparing to travel, I heard the same concerns—over and over again—about my safety. The damage I was doing to my marriage prospects was a close second. But, the driving force behind these questions was always love.

My parents grew up in a time when security was considered very important. They got this from their parents, who grew up just after WWII, a time of overwhelming uncertainty. As a result, my family greatly values safety, stability, and tradition.

But, today we live in a time of insecurity. There aren't many lifelong jobs, no guaranteed state pensions, healthcare is a lottery, and the only thing we know for sure is that you never know what tomorrow will bring. As a result, we're more likely to value flexibility, adaptability, and risk.

Our parents lived for the future and saved for a rainy day. We live in the present and save for experiences we can't get at home.

I know I'm generalizing here, but dealing with the reactions of your family and friends is going to be one of the most challenging and emotionally draining parts of this journey. Unlike other aspects of the process, this won't stop when you board the plane.

When you're on the road, your family will never stop being concerned for you, either. My Dad didn't sleep soundly for the full two months I lived in the capital of Colombia, Bogota. You need to learn to deal with this emotional hurdle without further upsetting them (like avoiding their calls would do) while protecting yourself from their negative perception of your life choices.

My parents have never told me that they outright disapprove of my lifestyle. But it cuts me deep every time my mum utters the words, "I just wish you would meet someone, settle in one place, and be happy." Sadly, my mum believes that happiness is attainable only when you're in a stable relationship and own your own home. She can't quite understand how any person (never mind her own daughter) could find happiness living out of a suitcase and traveling to a new country every few months. Does that mean she isn't proud of me? Does that mean she doesn't express love and support? No. But, it's still hard for my mum to understand the appeal of the nomad lifestyle. I have learned to respect her position, as she is respectful of my decisions.

The process of telling your loved ones about your decision to go nomadic and responding to their ongoing concerns as you travel will go more smoothly if you can empathize with them, even when they're showering you in negativity. At the core, all of us want to feel heard. So, listen, reassure them, and let it go.

Do not—I repeat—*do not* take on their fears as your own. Separate your feelings and emotions from those of your family. It's okay for them to have concerns while you continue to follow through with your plan.

When I announced I was moving to Colombia, I could feel my mum's anxiety through the phone. She did not want me to go there. In fact, she was terrified. Why? Because *she* would be scared to go there. Mum hasn't sat in a hostel talking to backpackers who gush about the beauty of Colombia's landscape, how friendly the people are, and how Medellín is the next digital nomad hotspot complete with a thriving coworking space. Mum doesn't speak Spanish. In fact, at this point, she had never stepped foot in Latin America because the media told her it's unsafe. Is it really surprising that she doesn't want her daughter traveling alone to a country renowned for kidnappings and cocaine?

I could have argued with her and used all of my mental energy trying to persuade her that I'd be fine. I could have sent her articles that reveal why Colombia is an amazing place to visit, in an effort to change her decades-old opinion. But, this would have put a strain on our relationship and made me want to avoid talking to her. Or I could have adopted her fears as my own, which probably would have stopped me from going to Colombia.

Instead, I reassured my mum that I know what I'm doing and I will be careful. And I've accepted that a mother — mine or yours — is never going to stop worrying about their child, no matter where that grown-ass adult is living.

If the fears of your family and friends start to feel like your own anxieties, try this. Turn to those who have been there: your new community, your tribe of travelers. Post a comment or question in one of the solo female travel forums on social media. Ask the women who have actually visited or lived in these "scary" places what you should be aware of and how to best prepare yourself to go there. They can offer reality-based insight, support, and reassurance in a way your family probably can't.

To get through this while keeping your family and friendship ties intact, you need to develop a thick skin and learn to balance their negativity with positivity (both internal and externally from other female travelers).

I receive emails all the time from solo female travelers planning to go to Guatemala who are freaking out because their parents are freaking out. These girls find my blog and thank me for reassuring them it's safe to go alone. I always respond, and I'm happy to help. That's how most of the nomad community operates. So, don't be too intimidated to reach out to bloggers. We were all where you are once.

Fast forward. More than three years later, my family and I have adopted a don't-ask-don't-tell policy. I tell my mum when I'm on the move and when good things happen that I want to share. I just skip over most of the bad stuff. She doesn't need to know all of the details of her wayward daughter's life.

Tips for dealing with over-anxious friends and family:

Try to have a respectful conversation with them. Ask your inner circle what it would take for them to worry less. Maybe they want a daily text or weekly phone calls. Whatever it is, respect it and try to honor it. If you really want to try to make them understand what you're doing and why, send them positive articles from solo female travelers. It may just do the trick.

Whatever you do, don't read all of the fear-inducing articles and news stories they may send you. Seriously. Don't do it! Being prepared is one thing; freaking yourself out reading 10-year-old stories of kidnapped tourists is quite another.

If they won't listen to you, you can't make them, and trying to do so is going to drive you crazy. So just don't. Smile, tell them you hear their concerns and you understand their fears. Tell them you will stay in touch and you will not take risks. Then surround yourself with the positive voices in your life.

Watch (re-watch?) *Eat Pray Love*, read the memoir *Wild*, stalk your favorite solo female travelers on Instagram. Make lists of places you're going to see, activities you want to try, and personal and professional goals you aim to reach while traveling. Do what you need to do to feel inspired and optimistic again.

Most of my friends and family were almost as excited as I was about my decision to travel fulltime. They admired my bravery and appreciated my sense of adventure. They genuinely wanted to know about my plans and asked me if I was nervous, rather than telling me I should be scared. Gravitate to these kinds of people in your life. You're going to need cheerleaders in your corner.

Dealing with negativity from friends and family can be exhausting, especially when you see them in person regularly. Once you start traveling, it will get easier. You'll meet other women travelers who have dealt with the same thing. Your family will see your Facebook photos and status updates, and they'll soon realize how happy you are and back off.

I've been on the road for over three years now, and I know my family won't stop worrying. But they've also come to respect my decision. They know that I'm living how I want to live, and most importantly, that I'm happier because of it.

Solo Traveling Over 30

If you've outgrown your 20s, you may be wondering if this kind of lifestyle is for you. I see many women in their 30s, 40s, 50s, and beyond asking the digital nomad Facebook groups if there's anyone "their age" doing this. There's a lot of visual representation of 20-somethings living the digital nomad life. They're the pretty people flooding social media with #livingmybestlife. Even mainstream news outlets are aiming their cameras at young, location-independent professionals. There's less coverage and self-promotion of more mature female solo travelers.

Let me set the record straight. There are an abundance of women in their 30s, 40s, and 50s living this lifestyle. Some solo, some with friends, others as part of a couple, and many with young families. Some of these women have been traveling for a decade. But, many of them made a big decision to uproot the stable lives they spent years building to ride this digital nomad wave. Maybe they aren't posting about it on Instagram every five minutes for their 17.5K followers, but they're out there living their best lives, believe me.

Female travelers over 30 often have different needs, concerns, and expectations than their younger counterparts.

Maybe you don't want to stay in hostels because you'll be forced to hang out with teenage backpackers every night. Well, just avoid the party hostels, and you might be surprised how civilized and stylish today's hostels can be.

Maybe you're not sure how to meet other like-minded travelers and make new friends. I can't say this enough—join the city-specific DN Facebook groups! You'll see people posting about local networking and social events, and making plans to co-work in local cafés. You can also join Couchsurfing. Even if you never want to crash on someone's couch, this app is a good way to connect with expats, other travelers, and locals (many of whom host casual get-togethers). Join Meetup to meet locals and other DNs who share your interests and hobbies. If you join Nomad List, it has a function that shows you other members staying in your city – and lets you chat with members in Slack groups organized by city and interest/activity.

Another way to meet people is through Airbnb Experiences. For a fee, you can participate in an organized group activity like hiking, making art, cooking a local dish, attending an intimate concert by local musicians, or going on a bike tour hosted by a local. You can also attend social and networking events hosted by local co-working spaces. Usually, they promote these on their Facebook pages.

I'm always surprised by the wide age range of people I meet in real life through these apps and websites.

If you're still worried that you're too old for this, let me tell you something.

At 34, I was much wiser and savvier than I was at 24. I had no hesitation about my ability to survive alone in a foreign country and stay safe. Having spent the better part of 10 years developing my skills in the workplace, I had a broad and varied skillset, including a lot of leadership experience. My CV at 24 wasn't that impressive. When I was in my 20s, it would have been a lot harder for me to make this switch and earn the money I'm currently earning. At 34, however, I was under no illusions about what I was leaving behind, what I would gain, and what I would have to sacrifice to become a fulltime traveler. This perspective comes only with age and experience.

Don't conclude that just because you're over 30 this is going to be harder for you. In reality, becoming a successful digital nomad is more attainable for you now than it was for your younger self.

Speech over.

Now that we've covered the emotional and physical challenges of becoming a digital nomad, it's time to get down to the nitty gritty.

Chapter 4 - Money

One thing I learned as a producer is you have to start with the money!

Remember: You are never going to feel like you have enough money to travel fulltime. If you're waiting for the perfect number to appear in your savings account, you will never leave.

This is the time to dig out your bank statements, credit card bills, student loan statements, and all of your other financial stuff. Spend some time going through everything. You need to face the reality about four things:

1. How much money you have
2. How much money you owe
3. How much time you have before you leave
4. How much money you can save in that time

By the time you hit the road, you should be earning enough from working remotely that your savings are just for unexpected/big expenses and emergencies

When I first left home, I had enough work lined up for the coming months to give me a modest income. But for that first year while I was building up my Freelance writing income, I taught Chinese children English online. If I'm honest, I hated it. I especially disliked the 4am wakeups thanks to the time difference. But it gave me a steady income that helped support me while I built up enough writing work so that I could quit. Now I have several passive income streams thanks to the books I have written and the affiliate marketing money I make from my blog. It's not enough to live off, but it keeps me going if I have a quiet month or want to take time off for traveling.

Saving money vs. paying off your debts

When I left for Guatemala, I had only $1000 in savings. But, I had paid off my debts.

If you have to prioritize financial goals, I think it's better to pay off your debts. Saving a bit of money while swimming in debt isn't going to help in the long term. Having paid off or significantly paid down your debt before you start traveling will reduce your stress and make fulltime travel more sustainable long-term.

When I sold everything I didn't need to take with me on my travels, I put every penny of the profits toward clearing my debts. After that, I started contributing to my savings account. Although I often felt sad about selling my things, watching my bank balance steadily increase was the best feeling.

When it comes to start-up money, you have two options:

Option 1 - Save enough money that you don't have to work at the very start of your trip, or you have to work only a few hours each week to get by. This will free up your time and mental energy so you can focus on traveling to new destinations. You can also use your free time to develop or advance your remote-work skills so you can start taking on jobs when your money runs low.

Option 2 - Save as much money as you can so you have a buffer to get you through any tough months as a digital nomad. Or, you can use this money for more expensive trips, like the Inca Trail or a scuba diving course.

How's this for motivation to save your money?

1 mojito in the UK = £7
1 mojito in NYC = $12
1 mojito in Guatemala = less than $1

For each drink you don't have at home, you can have 12 when you're abroad. BOOM!

My top money-saving tips

1. Get a piggy bank.

Honestly, do it. Not one that you can dip into for bus money. Get one that you would have to smash to get into it! I save only £2 coins, and my piggy bank holds over £1000 when full. Start saving a year in advance of your travels.

Another option is to hand over your money to someone who you trust more than yourself. For a year, I sent money each month to my dad for safekeeping. I gave him strict instructions to allow me to dip into my own savings only under certain circumstances. Doing this will ensure you don't have a bad day and blow your hard-earned savings on cute boots or a new camera lens you don't really need.

2. Don't party so hard.

You'll be tempted to go out with friends for brunches and happy hours in the months leading up to your departure. But, you've got to keep your goals in mind. Try having girls' nights in instead. Become the most reliable designated driver this year! Or, find ways to spend time with your friends that doesn't involve spending money. You'll have plenty of opportunities to party as a traveler. But now's the time for eliminating non-essential spending so you can pay down your debt and put money into savings.

3. Reduce your monthly recurring bills.

While it may feel like Netflix is essential to sustain human life, consider this one of your monthly expenses that you should probably eliminate. I recommend canceling all paid subscriptions (digital music, cable TV, podcasts, magazines, food delivery services) and giving up beauty services (manicures and pedis, those pretty balayage treatments, facials, blow outs, brow treatments) as much as you can get away with. By doing so, I was able to save over £100 every month, which is enough for a dorm bed for 3 weeks in Thailand.

4. Re-evaluate your wardrobe.

A year before I started traveling, I stopped spending money on special occasion dresses, heels, purses, jewelry, and random pieces I used to treat myself to every now and then. These items aren't necessary while you're traveling, so you won't need them. When I did buy something new, it would have to be purposeful and practical for my new life as a traveler. Every article of clothing/shoes you pack should to be comfortable, versatile, small/lightweight, and easy to wash (no dry cleaning and preferably no ironing required).

It's a personal choice, but I'd rather spend my money on adventures than designer clothing. Dressing well may be more important to you now, but you'll find that the nomad community dresses casually, and if you suddenly need a new sundress and sandals for a date, they won't be too hard to find, regardless of where you are.

5. Cook more often and avoid dining out.

For me, this piece of advice was the most difficult to follow. My lifestyle was hectic, and my productivity requires too many caffeinated drinks to get me through the day. In a world without Netflix, partying, and retail therapy, I deserved my daily coffee fix, goddammit! But really, I didn't. And giving up that convenience was the easiest way I found to save some serious money.

If you're similarly in the habit of treating yourself to pricey prepared coffees, cold pressed juices, sushi, brunches, or whatever, find practical ways to break that addiction now. Keep in mind, you're making these sacrifices today so you can enjoy far cheaper cappuccinos and açaí bowls in Bali tomorrow.

6. Start collecting air miles.

This tip requires spending money in the right way so you can save money later. There are a few credit cards available that offer discounts on travel expenses (like flights, insurance, and hotels) or enable you to earn air miles by making purchases. Do your research and sign up for at least one credit card that you can use to buy groceries, gas, and all your necessities. It's not an excuse to purchase non-essentials, rather a great way to reduce the money you'll spend on flights. In the UK, it's not easy to get lots of air miles from credit cards, but there are ways. I had a Nectar card that can pay for flights with EasyJet, and my Tesco Club card points automatically got converted into Virgin Airlines miles.

Before you start flying, sign up for an account with each airline that offers a reward membership program. Keep an eye out for flash sales on flights and offers to earn extra points. It all adds up, and you can use your points to purchase discounted or free flights.

If you're from the U.S., you need to learn about travel hacking. Nomadic Matt is the king of this practice, and I highly recommend you learn the tricks of this trade from his website www.nomadicmatt.com or his book.

7. Set a date and book the flight!

Even if it means you will be a bit short that month, there is no greater incentive for saving money than actually having something to look forward to. With a date circled on your calendar and a plane ticket in hand, you'll find the strength to turn down an invitation to go to the movies, leave the cute boots at the store, and eat your homemade salad for lunch.

Chapter 5 - Finding a Digital Nomad Job

This part is easier for some than others. In fact, you may want to just skip this chapter if you already have a remote job lined up or can transition your current job into a remote position. You can return to this chapter at another time, when you want or need to change the nature of your professional life.

But, if you're like many people (including me), you'll completely change your career when you become a digital nomad. And you might not have figured out yet what your new work life will look like.

Before I went nomadic, I was the director of a UK based dance company, not something I could do from a beach in Bali. Figuring out how I would earn an income while traveling fulltime didn't happen overnight.

What kind of location-independent professional will you be?

Those who work while they travel fulltime generally fall into these categories:

Remote employees typically work full-time for a company or organization. But they can work from home, wherever that may be. As a remote worker, you may have to be at your computer or on your phone during normal working hours wherever your employer is based. This can be an issue if you're, say, working for a New York-based marketing agency while living 12 hours ahead in Thailand. But if you can set your own hours, you can finish a day's work from a café in Barcelona before your supervisor back home pours their first cup of coffee.

Remote employees who temporarily live in a different city or country than where their employers are based are most likely **digital nomads**. Such jobs include software engineer, social media manager, writer, graphic/web designer, and online educator.

But some remote employees aren't digital nomads. Yet they still have the freedom to live and work from locations around the world. These professionals work fulltime for a company or organization that serves the communities where the remote employee visits or lives. Such jobs include healthcare providers, medical researchers, environmental activists and researchers, and those working for companies seeking to expand their business in foreign countries.

Freelancers are self-employed people who sell their services to others or run their own business. I fit into this category because I earn money as a freelance copywriter, SEO/SEM wiz, and blogger. But you can be a freelancer without being a digital nomad. Your profitable service may be teaching classes/lessons, hosting workshops or events, photography, doing hair/makeup, pet sitting, childcare, cooking, gardening, or performing in the locations you visit as a traveler.

Location-independent professionals often work as much or as hard as people with "normal" jobs. We just have more control over when and where we work. Some weeks, I work more than 12 hours a day to get through my workload so I can disappear for a few days into a South American jungle or European city. Other weeks, I work just a few hours a day.

How easy is it to become a digital nomad?

This really depends on you and your career history. If you went directly from college into a 9 to 5 corporate job, you might have a steep learning curve. If you're freelancing or self-employed, you already have many of the skills you need to succeed as a digital nomad.

Becoming a digital nomad wasn't a difficult transition for me. I was used to working from home as a dance producer. While I attended plenty of meetings and events, I did my actual work from home, our company office, or a café.

But no one was going to just hand me a remote position. So I created one for myself.

I figured out which parts of my job I could do as a freelancer living abroad. As a producer, I did everything from copywriting to basic graphic design. Plus, I had experience building websites and managing social media.

I came up with a solid concept and logistics for my new role as a location-independent freelancer, and I pitched it to my colleagues and supervisors. I explained that I could continue working for them without ever physically being there. My biggest concern was persuading the companies I worked for that I could do the same job at the same level of quality while living in a different time zone. Luckily, my former employers all agreed to become my first freelance clients (on a trial basis). This meant I had secured half of my monthly income for my first six months of travel.

If this kind of transition is an option for you, I strongly suggest exploring it. Moving your current job to a remote location is the quickest and easiest way to enter the nomadic lifestyle without starting from scratch.

I also started a blog that I hoped would grow over time to provide me with a more passive income stream through affiliate marketing. Alongside this, I managed social media for two companies I worked with, and I continued to write funding applications and manage tours for two other companies. To advance my skills, I took a course on social media management. The companies were happy for me to learn on the job because I already had a relationship with them.

Three years later, I'm not doing any of these jobs, but they helped me get through my first year as a nomad without starving.

If taking some aspects of your current job on the road with you isn't going to work, then I recommend you figure out what kind of work you can do from your computer and phone.

The first thing you should decide is if you want to be a self-employed freelancer or a full-time remote employee. If it is the latter, then you need time to job hunt and apply for remote positions. If you decide to go it alone, you need to offer a marketable skill or service.

Start by asking yourself the following questions:

> Do I have strong IT skills, including web design, graphics, or coding?
> Do I have excellent writing skills and experience as a copywriter or journalist?
> Do I have the qualifications to teach English as a foreign language?
> Do I have experience in marketing?
> Do I have strong administrative skills?
> Are there any responsibilities in my current job that I could effectively manage for clients while living in another city or country?

If you answered yes to any of the above then there's a very good chance you could do one of these common Digital Nomad jobs.

- web designer
- graphic designer
- app developer
- writer: copywriter, technical writer, travel writer, editor
- online English teacher
- marketing and PR consultancy
- social media manager
- virtual assistant
- blogger, vlogger, social media influencer
- SEO/SEM expert

Whatever you decide to pursue, the likelihood is you'll need some kind of online training course. During my first two years, I took so many courses, I lost count. But I also learned a lot from the work itself. Since becoming a digital nomad, my work has grown and evolved. I stopped accepting the clients and jobs I didn't like and learned how to find and secure the kinds of jobs I wanted. If I found a skills gap, I took a course to fill the gap.

Digital Nomad Courses

Here's a list of my favorite courses that I found most helpful:

Web Design | App Development | Graphic Design

For any kind of coding or design courses, I recommend skillcrush.com, which is led by women for women to help you break into tech. They offer lots of free resources so you can see if it's right for you before committing. They also have payment plans.

Copywriting | Technical Writing | Travel Writing
Udemy has some great copywriting courses. If you're interested in becoming a travel writer, I recommend a course offered by Nomadic Matt in his online Superstar Blogger School the price used to be almost $300 but he has reduced all his courses to just $99.

Teaching English Online
You really don't need a course for this; just check out YouTube. Plenty of teachers have made great videos to help you with your interview and teaching tips. If you can secure your TEFL credentials, you'll probably earn more money as a teacher.

Marketing | PR Consultancy | Social Media Management

I've not done it personally, but I have heard amazing things about The Digital Gangster Course from a lot of other female digital nomads. It's not the cheapest course around but it is the best, and you get what you pay for!

I've also heard great things about the Bucket list Bombshells courses.

Virtual Assistant

Check out digitalnomadkit.com. The founder is a total badass and runs an amazing Facebook group. There are plenty of free resources for aspiring VAs, but if you're serious, I recommend her course, as it will teach you everything you need to know.

Blogger | Vlogger | Influencer

There are so many courses by so-called influencers. But the only one I recommend is The Business of Blogging by Nomadic Matt. If you're going to take a blogging course, go to the man who pretty much started it all. I have taken this course, and it changed the way I blog. I finally started making money from my blog after implementing what I learned in Nomadic Matt's course. If vlogging is your thing, he also has a vlogging course put together by Nadine and Sarah — two awesome vloggers. I have also taken this course and highly recommend it. Both of these courses are worth every penny.

My full review of these courses is available on my blog: clairesitchyfeet.com/online-blogging-courses.

SEO/SEM

I teach SEO, and conduct SEO audits and work on websites as a part of my remote work. But I can't say that any one course taught me everything I needed to know. I learned a lot from Nomadic Matt's course The Business of Blogging. Then I discovered DNW (Digital Nomad Wannabe), who is the queen of SEO as far as I'm concerned! Join her Facebook group, sign up for her newsletter, and take her course if you want a fast track to learning SEO.

For SEM, there is only one course worth taking, and it's super cheap! But the course is long and the information is a lot to wrap your head around. It's called Ultimate Google Ads/AdWords Course 2018 (by Isaac Rudansky). This course is so detailed and in depth, it will teach you everything you need to know to get started. I would recommend having a solid understanding of SEO before you take this course.

Skillshare

One of my favorite online resources is Skillshare. They have tens of thousands of courses on everything from photography to marketing. If you sign up using the link on my website you can get 2 months.

To read my full list of Digital Nomad Resources visit my blog clairesitchyfeet.com/resources/digital-nomad-resources/

Digital Nomad Job/Gig Hunting

Once you've figured out what you want to do and learned from a course or two, start looking for jobs! The most common places to find jobs are online freelance websites, Facebook groups, and word of mouth. Most of the work I've secured as a freelancer I found through a friend, former colleague, or personal contact. I've been lucky that people tend to seek me out, or I meet them in person while traveling, then we end up working together. This is the case for all of my current clients.

Develop some serious networking skills. Learn how to effectively pitch and sell yourself to potential clients and how to ask for the money you deserve. These are often big sticking points for women, so it is good to develop these skills early on. Be confident in your abilities, and don't ever let a client pay you less than your worth. You may need to do some free or discounted work when you're starting out, but you can't sustain that long term.

Print business cards, set up a simple website where you can showcase your skills and portfolio, and join some female-only Facebook groups. I prefer these groups because they're more supportive. There are always opportunities for collaborating and finding new clients.

Digital Nomad Resources

If you haven't already started reading self-improvement books for entrepreneurs, I recommend you start now. The messaging and soft skills you can learn from the pros will help put you in the right mindset and improve your professional confidence. Even if you've never considered yourself to be a business-minded person, now's the time to start thinking and acting like an entrepreneur. Being a freelancer is exactly that: a corporation of one.

My self-improvement reading list (this list is made up of a mix of self-help, inspirational, and spiritual reads that I've read myself, or am currently reading):

You are a Badass: How to Stop Doubting Your Greatness and Start Living an Awesome Life by Jen Sincero

The Art of Thinking Clearly by Rolf Dobelli

Start with Why by Simon Sinek

You Are a Badass at Making Money: Master the Mindset of Wealth by Jen Sincero

The Happiness of Pursuit: Finding the Quest That Will Bring Purpose to Your Life by Chris Guillebeau

Unfu*k Yourself: Get Out of Your Head and Into Your Life by Gary John Bishop

The Alchemist by Paulo Coelho

The Power of Vulnerability by Brene Brown (in fact anything Brene Brown writes you should read)

The 4-Hour Workweek by Tim Ferriss

Women who Run with the Wolves: Myths and Stories of the Wild Woman Archetype by Clarissa Pinkola Estés

Wild: From Lost to Found on the Pacific Crest Trail by Cheryl Strayed

Designing Your Life: How to Build a Well-lived, Joyful Life by Bill Burnett, Dave Evans, and David John Evans

Be a Free Range Human: Escape the 9-5, Create a Life You Love and Still Pay the Bills by Marianne Cantwell

The 7 Habits of Highly Effective People by Stephen Covey

The Power of Habit by Charles Duhigg
The Artist's Way by Julia Cameron
The Subtle Art of Not Giving a F*ck by Mark Manson
Vagabonding by Rolf Potts
The Element: How Finding Your Passion Changes Everything by Ken Robinson
Big Magic by Elizabeth Gilbert

Websites for searching and applying for freelance jobs:
www.itsatravelod.com/find-remote-jobs
www.fiverr.com
www.flexjobs.com/
remoters.net/
www.workingnomads.co/jobs
www.upwork.com/
www.facebook.com/groups/DigitalNomadJobs/
www.facebook.com/groups/remotejobsfordigitalnomads/

Facebook groups that support digital nomads, freelancers, and female entrepreneurs:
Female Digital Nomads
www.facebook.com/groups/1607248466232418/
Digital Nomad Girls
www.facebook.com/groups/DigitalNomadGirls/
Digital Nomads Tribe Playa del Carmen
www.facebook.com/groups/272902926906743
Digital Nomad Wannabe
www.facebook.com/DigitalNomadWannabe/

An outstanding resource (who happens to be a good friend of mine) is Andrea Valeria. She offers a course worth taking if you want to learn more about a variety of digital nomad jobs and unique income streams. She often posts about remote jobs on her Instagram stories. Plus, she wrote a step-by-step book about starting and monetizing your own vlog.

You can find her over at It's a Travel OD
www.itsatravelod.com/

For my full list of Digital Nomad Recourses visit my website
clairesitchyfeet.com/resources/digital-nomad-resources/

Chapter 6 - Show Me The Money

The key to being a successful digital nomad is balance: balance your time and energy while also keeping your bank balance looking healthy. Take it from someone who arrived in Bogota with $50 in her pocket and no payday in sight, you do NOT want to run out of money on the road (especially while living in one of the most dangerous cities in the world, but that's a story for another book).

It can be easy to choose tacos and margaritas on the beach with friends over a day stuck inside with only your laptop for company. But the only way you can really enjoy time off is by ensuring you're also doing enough work to pay for those margaritas. You'll have to sacrifice some adventures and locales simply because they don't have reliable Wi-Fi. Without Wi-Fi, most digital nomads can't work.

You need to learn the art of work-life balance.

The first step towards this is taking charge of your finances. I discussed how to save money in Chapter 4, and pointed out that you don't need a huge savings account. But you will need a decent buffer in case a client delays paying you or you lose a client unexpectedly. Most importantly, you need a solid idea of how much monthly income you need to cover living and travel expenses.

Financial stability is tricky for freelancers. The best piece of advice I can give you is to generate several income streams. Make sure the bulk of your money isn't coming from a single source. As a freelancer, your clients come and go, often with little notice. If a client leaves, you need to be able to survive without them until you can find a new client to replace them.

Ideally, you want to have enough money in your account for three months of expenses and a plane ticket home. For many DNs, $4,000 (USD) would be ideal. But, I had $1,000 (USD) to my name when I started out as a nomad three years ago, and I've scraped by — even though I often scraped a bit too close to the curb!

It's time to make some financial projections.

Let's say you know which country or continent you want to live in. Do your research and ask other nomads what things generally cost there. Consider your accommodations, groceries, local transportation, coworking space fees, dining out/cocktails/coffee shops, laundry services, toiletries and cosmetics, wellness expenses like a gym or yoga studio membership, clothes/shoes, medical expenses like prescriptions and doctor visits, and entertainment (concerts, nature or adventure tours, water sports, museums).

Don't forget to account for other expenses like your cell phone bill, health or travel insurance, or any digital subscriptions or services you need while traveling. Create a monthly budget for living in this place you've got your heart set on. Then add a little extra money to that number for income taxes, unforeseen expenses, and emergencies (like a busted computer!) because, let's be real. That's how much income you must earn each month from your location-independent employment to make this work. Until you know you can earn this minimum amount, it is unadvisable to risk traveling fulltime.

That said, if you're a bit of a risk-taker (like me) and work better under pressure, book the ticket and you will figure it out. Or, you'll end up living off bread and eggs for a few months like I did in Bogota. (Although, I really wouldn't advise this. It was awful).

If you aren't sure where you want to travel to first, start by nailing down your monthly income. Once you know how much money you have at your disposal, you can look for a destination to match your budget. If you know you won't be earning much and need to ensure a low cost of living, Latin America and South East Asia are your best options, as your money will go a lot farther.

After you've determined a monthly budget, put your energies into finding and securing enough regular, reliable work and passive income to cover your expenses and grow your savings account. You can't achieve a good work-life balance without a steady income.

The next step is to set some deadlines for yourself.

Put your "I'm outta here" date on the calendar. I think this is essential to keep you on track.

You know how much money you need to save and earn to get started, so set a realistic but motivating deadline for reaching that number.

Set a deadline for buying your plane ticket.

Make another deadline for getting your affairs in order (selling and donating your belongings and your car, subletting your apartment, and making any necessary changes to your cell phone plan and health insurance).

I gave myself six months to reach these deadlines. You may need a year. If you already have a remote job or passive income, you may need just a couple months to sort out a few details. The timeline really depends on your unique situation and determination.

Chapter 7 - Planning

If there's one thing that my time on the road has taught me, it's that life has a habit of throwing you a curveball when you least expect it. Does that mean planning is a waste of time? Quite the opposite, if you ask me. I say, over-plan.

Make to-do lists and spreadsheets. Pin everything on Google Maps, from touristy vistas to your new local grocery store. Create boards on Pinterest to save travel hacks, dream destinations, and that perfect backpack. Ask as many questions as you can think of in travel Facebook groups. Color-code your Google Docs.

You are embarking on a HUGE life change. This over-planning will help calm your nerves, give you something to look forward to, and fill your time while you have no social life thanks to all the money-saving you're doing.

Any successful long-term traveler will probably tell you that they planned a lot in the beginning. They will also tell you that they often threw that plan out the window as soon as something way cooler came up. That's fine, too. But you're going to be prepared and ready for the unexpected.

Part of the joy of this lifestyle is that you're choosing to free yourself from the normal adult life constraints. So, don't be afraid to be impulsive. It's likely that you'll meet someone who tells you about this really cool place that isn't on your itinerary, and you find yourself on a road-trip with them the following weekend. Or you may arrive in a city you couldn't wait to visit only to learn that it's not a good match for you. Or, you land a new client and need to hunker down and get to work for a couple weeks instead of going on that wilderness excursion you planned for.

You'll find that you just can't make an iron-tight plan and stick to it. Planning for this lifestyle isn't the same as scheduling every hour of a weeklong vacation. Plan as much as you need for you to feel in control and safe. Planning will also empower you to make informed decisions about where you go, how long you stay, and doing so within your budget.

As a digital nomad, you'll have to plan a little differently than you're accustomed to; however, this lifestyle will offer you a lot more freedom than your average cubical-dwelling 9 to 5 role, but you still have some constraints…

Wi-Fi
Wi-Fi
Wi-Fi
And your speed of travel

Solid Wi-Fi is a deal breaker because you can't work without it. Sure, you can get by without Wi-Fi for a long weekend if you worked ahead and scheduled the time off. And, if you have an off-line portion of your job, you can handle that when you're off the grid for few days. As long as you communicate with your clients/employer and let them know when you will and won't be available, it shouldn't be a problem.

But if you need to respond to frequent emails, teach online, make video calls, or upload and download large files, you should ask your accommodations host to run a Wi-Fi speed test and share the results with you before you commit to staying there. I also recommend getting a backup hotspot. I've been to places where I wanted to stay for weeks, but had to leave after two days because the Wi-Fi was so weak. Generally, you will have to make your travel plans around locations, Airbnbs, coffee shops, and even buses/trains with Wi-Fi.

The other major thing you're going to have to account for is your travel speed. You may want to see all of South America in three months, but that would involve traveling to a new place every few days. While this is something a backpacker may be able to accomplish while enjoying their gap year, as a digital nomad, you're going to need to slow down your pace … a lot.

Determining the right speed of travel for you, your work, and your budget will be a matter of trial and error. I prefer moving slowly. I stay in a country for months rather than weeks. When I arrived in Guatemala, I expected to be in Argentina within a year and cover most of the countries in between along the way. I ended up spending nine months in Guatemala and six months in Colombia with a few short trips sprinkled in.

Other DNs prefer to move every three or four weeks. Most likely, when you get started on your journey, you will want to move frequently from city to city or from one country to the next. What typically happens is the fast pace leads to mental/emotional burnout and physical fatigue/illness. Or, you'll miss a few work deadlines then realize you need to slow down. It's a rite of passage for all digital nomads. Over time, you'll figure out the best pace for you.

I now average moving every two to six months, depending on how much I like a place. I don't just stay in one place for six months, though. I rent an apartment, and every couple of weeks, I pack my daypack and take off for a week or so to explore a nearby rural town or city without the burden of carrying all my possessions on my back. It is so much more pleasant to travel and explore with a daypack than a 20kg backpack plus day bag. But don't worry about this too much. You'll find your groove on the road.

Other than these two constraints, planning your DN lifestyle is a lot like planning for an extended travel adventure. If you've never planned a long trip (more than a week or two), this may seem overwhelming. No worries; I'm going to walk you step by step through my travel planning process.

4 Questions to Determine Where You're Headed

1 – What's in your wallet?
You should have already determined your projected monthly income by now. So, you already know how much you can afford to spend on living expenses and flights. If you haven't figured out this part yet, take a step back to review Chapter 6.

2 – You want to live the dream? What does that look like?

Close your eyes and imagine you're already there. Take some time to visualize the perfect destination, what activities you'll do there, what you will eat, which neighborhood you'll live in, and the style of accommodations you prefer. What kind of work environment do you want to be in (coworking space, home office, poolside, or coffee shop)? Do you want to be surrounded by other digital nomads, or do you want to be somewhere off the beaten path? Take your time and let your mind wander until you find yourself in the perfect environment for you to work and enjoy during your time off.

One of the most important things to consider is if you want to be hot or cold. Depending on your preference, you are instantly going to rule out certain regions of the world. If you want sunny beaches and humid jungles, then forget most of Europe for much of the year. If you envision yourself happily bundled up with a scarf and enjoying a snowy hike in the mountains stay away from countries close to the equator. But remember, this isn't just a vacation! You're going to need to work and go grocery shopping and exercise and do your laundry. Can you handle all of that in the sweltering heat, frigid cold, or during monsoon season?

3 – What is there to do in paradise?
What kind of activities do you love? Scuba diving, hiking, making art or music, kickboxing, yoga, sailing? Do you want to volunteer in the local community or learn a new language? Are you looking for a quiet place to meditate or write? Or do you need an active nightlife scene to be happy?

Write down all of your priorities (remember your budget!), and get Googling to find some Wi-Fi-friendly destinations that meet your needs. Don't hesitate to ask those Facebook groups for advice. They may have some great ideas that you hadn't even thought of.

4 – So, where are you going?
I'm not going to lie, I often choose my next destination with a little help from Skyscanner, Hopper, or Scotts Cheap Flights. I enter my airport, choose "anywhere in the world," and filter it so the cheapest flights are displayed first. Then, I research the countries with the least expensive flights and pick my favorite. I don't let myself be picky about flight times and layovers. The more flexible you are with flights, the more money you can save on the way to your next destination. If you want your money to last longer, you need to get good at finding cheap flights unless you can reach your next destination by bus or train (especially if you're moving around Europe).

Make a list of your top five destinations based on your interests, your budget, the estimated cost of living, the weather, Wi-Fi availability, safety, and the cheap flights you found. Now pick one and buy that ticket!

More Questions to Answer Before You Leave

1 – What's in the fine print?
Once you decide on your next location, you still have a bunch of research to do. I always look up the following:

- Best accommodations within my budget (very important)
- Sights to see
- Things to do
- Where and what to eat
- Where to get work done/which places have good Wi-Fi
- Where to exercise (if you're looking for a gym, yoga classes, or dance studio)
- Any neighborhoods to avoid because they're considered unsafe
- Local cultural norms/taboos

Nomad List is a great resource for researching digital nomad-friendly cities. I'm also a big fan of Pinterest, which I use to pin things to my country- and city-specific boards. When used right, Pinterest can be a total game changer and every traveler's best friend.

2 – Where are you going to live?
Other than picking a destination, deciding where to live is the hardest part. To get started, I simply Google "where to stay" or "best places to stay" in my desired city. When you find places that you like, add them to your Pinterest board.

Each nomad-friendly city has its own Facebook group and Nomad List group consisting of people already living there and those who have stayed there in the past. They can tell you the best way to find local accommodations. Some cities have a local website full of short- and long-term listings. There are also Facebook groups designed to help digital nomads find housing by putting locals in touch with travelers interested in taking over their leases short term. Also, a number of co-living homes designed with nomads in mind are popping up around the world. I recommend asking the Facebook groups about standard local practices like deposits, contracts, Wi-Fi, and safe neighborhoods. These groups have been a life saver for me and are always a wealth of information.

As a rule, I book only one or two nights in hotel or hostel before I arrive in a new place. Once I'm there, I look for somewhere to stay more long term. The price of accommodations typically goes down as you get closer to your arrival date. The exception is if there's a big event in the area. If that's the case, the earlier you book, the better.

Airbnb can be a good option, but it's not going to be the cheapest. Every time I've booked my accommodations on Airbnb for a month or more before actually visiting the place, I have regretted it. This is mostly because I ended up staying in an unsafe area, but also because of how much more expensive it was. One trick I do is search on Airbnb, make contact with the host outside the Airbnb site/app (via WhatsApp usually), and work out a better deal for my stay. Sometimes hosts are happy to do this so they don't have to give Airbnb a commission. If you are already in the area, you can ask to see the property and then make a face to face deal. I've saved hundreds of dollars doing this.

Ensure that your home has a kitchen so you can cook for yourself. Going out for your morning coffee and dining out for every meal can get expensive. Not every place comes with a full kitchen, so double check on this before you book. Some places claim they have a kitchen, but it's just a mini-refrigerator and a hotplate.

As a solo female traveler, you also need to ensure that the entrance to your home is safe. When I lived in Bogotá, my door opened directly onto the street, and this was a source of angst for me every night. There were many times when I was too scared to open my door because there were people hanging around outside my place. So I would walk laps around the block until I felt safe to enter. Because I hadn't visited this place before I booked it, I ended up committed to two long months of Entry Anxiety.

3 – How will you get from the airport or bus/train station to your accommodations?

I always have my first night's accommodation booked, and I figure out ahead of time how to get from the airport or bus/train station to my accommodations safely and cheaply. Again, I am willing to sacrifice some of my time and convenience to take the cheaper option, which is something you should get used to doing.

When researching the best way to reach my accommodations, I rely on my fellow travel bloggers. They often reveal how much a taxi should cost or if Uber or a local bus is the cheapest option. If you're flying, you should also check out the airport's website to read their traveling to/from information.

Understand the public transport options (buses, metros/subways, and local trains) before you leave. Your accommodations' website should provide information about public transport costs, schedules, and pickup/drop off locations. Compare this to the costs for private options like taxis (including any airport fees), Uber (if it's offered there), or a rental car (if you need a car during your stay). Sometimes hotels and hostels offer free airport transfer on a van or bus, so ask ahead of time. If you're staying in an Airbnb, ask the host what option they recommend, how much it should cost, and how long that trip should take. Sometimes the best option is a combination, like taking a bus out of the airport then getting on the metro, then walking to your front door.

You might be used to saving such information on your phone, but I also keep handwritten notes handy in case my phone dies before I reach my accommodations. You'll want to have the name, address, and phone number of your accommodations with you at all times. Having a printed map with your accommodations marked may seem old school, but when your cell doesn't have service and you can't access Google Maps, you'll be happy to have that on hand. There are also apps that allow you to download a local map so you won't have to rely on phone service to view a map.

4 – Where are you going to work?
The quickest and easiest way to figure out the best work spots in town is to search on the local digital nomad Facebook groups. DNs are often posting about local cafés and coffee shops with the strongest, most reliable Wi-Fi, the most available outlets so you can plug in your laptop, and the best seating for hours of uninterrupted work. Once you've met other digital nomads, you'll see that they often plan casual co-working sessions/meetups at laptop-friendly locations. If you prefer to work in a co-working space, find out where they are and ask about free passes to try them out. If a co-working space is important to you, it's worth noting where they are before you commit to your accommodations so you can book something nearby. Some nomads prefer to work from home to avoid the distractions, noise, and unpredictability of working in a public place.

5 – What will you see and do?
I normally Google something like "Top 10 things to do" in my location or "must see ____" (if I'm interested in seeing the best local temples, caves, museums, or whatever). I skim through articles and blogs and save my top choices on my Pinboard. I make notes in my travel planner about things to keep in mind when visiting each attraction, such as the entry fee, the best time of day and day of the week to visit, what to bring with me (like water, sunscreen, a tote bag), and how to get there.

In my experience, the best place to search for things to do is on Pinterest itself. Start searching for the country or place and then click on the pictures you like. Go back later to read the articles. Don't forget to search for the best local foods and drinks and where to find them, so you don't miss any amazing gastronomical experiences!

6 – What should you do and avoid doing?
My last search is for do's and don'ts in that particular country and culture. I do a quick scan of local news and current affairs so I'm aware of anything that could impact my trip. Being aware of local customs and norms will help you be a culturally responsible traveler. I've found that doing so makes settling into my new location so much smoother. and helps you avoid embarrassing situations, getting ripped off, offending locals, and sticking out. If you're concerned about human rights, animal rights, environmental or indigenous rights, or other non-monetary issues, research before you go to determine the most responsible way to travel and live in your destination country.

Chapter 8 - Packing

My Packing Philosophy

If you'd have asked me a year ago, I would have told you to pack only the essentials, no luxury items. My first year of travel, I lived with very little. When you have to carry everything on your back, it makes you much more selective about what you take with you.

But over the years, my priorities have changed. My digital nomad journey began as an adventure I was trying out for a year and has transformed into the way I live. Now that this is my life, I don't want to live quite so humbly.

Don't get me wrong, I can slum it with the rest of the backpackers, and I regularly do. When I got back from nine days in Cuba, the few articles of clothing I took with me looked like they needed burning. Living like that is fine for a short time, because backpackers return to the creature comforts of home eventually. But I don't. I quite literally carry my home on my back. Because I move every three to six months now, I carry a little more baggage weight than I used to.

Over time, I've swapped out some of my khaki-colored clothes for pretty dresses. And – I can't believe I'm actually saying this – I now have a hairdryer and hair straighteners. Yes, that's right, I'm "backpacking" with a mini salon. Quite frankly, I don't give a hoot if anyone judges me for what I consider to be necessities for my happiness. I like to look like my "normal" self every now and again. It makes me feel good. I also lug around a yoga mat, a bag of crystals, and my tarot card deck. These are little luxuries I could live without, but I choose not to because having them makes me feel at home wherever I go.

It's not a bad idea to get some little luxuries for your temporary home, too. I lived with a lovely French girl in Colombia. She was a designer and convinced me to buy some fairy lights to hang over my bed and a cactus for my desk. At first, I fought against this idea because it just seemed like a waste of money, as I couldn't take these things with me when I left. But I'm glad I got them because they made me feel so much more at home during those few months. When I left Colombia, I passed them on to a friend who appreciated them just as much.

So, my point is (because there is a point), don't feel embarrassed about packing a few luxury things that make you feel at home and give you joy. Just pick things that aren't too large or heavy. After a year on the road, you'll be craving a few comfort items and things that make you smile. You can always leave stuff behind if it becomes too cumbersome.

As you travel, your relationship to material possessions will seriously shift. You'll lose things, forget things, break things, and if you're unlucky, you'll have things stolen. You may want to cry at the time of impact. But, you'll move on quickly and realize that you actually need very little to live a happy nomad life.

Packing Logistics

When I started out on the road, I did so with only a backpack and a day bag. Now, my luggage depends on where I'm moving to. Sometimes the backpack gets left behind in favor of a suitcase and a tote bag. Do what works best for you, and take into consideration how much you can physically lift, pull, and carry at the same time. There will be plenty of instances when there's no one around to help you schlep all of your stuff onto a bus or down the stairs to the metro.

Before I hit the road, I was overly concerned with what to pack. I can't even tell you how many articles I read, checklists I printed, and Amazon lists I had. I had so much advice, yet so little space in my backpack!

What to Pack

Here's my contribution to the world of packing lists.

STORAGE

Backpack/suitcase – Whether you choose a suitcase or a backpack is up to you. Just keep the airlines' checked baggage/carry-on luggage weight limits and size restrictions in mind.

Day pack – You must have a great daypack that's lightweight but sturdy enough for your laptop and comfortable on your shoulders and back. One size does not fit all. This is going to be your mobile office.

Packing Cubes – Not only will they help keep your backpack/suitcase organized, but they will help you fit in way more clothes. I know this seems counter-intuitive to add additional material into the equation, but every traveler who comes around to the magic of packing cubes never looks back.

Toiletry bag – If you're planning on staying in hostels, make sure it has a loop so you can hang it. I recommend getting a toiletry bag made of material that you can easily wash in the sink.

Laundry bag – You don't need anything fancy. Pack a lightweight bag that you can toss in with the laundry to keep it from smelling funky. Use it to store your dirty clothes and haul them to the laundromat. I use a large tote bag for this.

Reusable shopping bag – I have two of these that fold up so they fit into a pouch. I use them for grocery shopping.

ESSENTIALS

Sleeping bag liner – If you're staying in hostels, it's worth bringing one of these with you just in case the bed is dirty. I used mine quite a lot because I was cold at night.

Water bottle – Don't be that person drinking from recyclable plastic bottles all the time. You won't get many uses out of those, and you'll find that recycling isn't readily available in many parts of the world. Get a reusable bottle. I recommend investing in a double-lined one that will keep your water (or rosé) cool on the beach.

Towels – Get quick-dry, space-saving microfiber towels. One for the beach/bath and one for face/hands.

Locks – It's a good idea to keep a lock or two in your bag. I prefer combination locks so I don't have to worry about keys. If you stay at a hostel, you will need one for your locker.

Head torch – I'm an adventure girl, so I never travel without my head torch (or headlamp). If you explore any caves or hike up volcanos, then you will be glad you have one. If nothing else, it's good for getting home at night and reading in bed!

Earplugs – If you're staying in hostels, you'll need earplugs. If not, it's still a good to have earplugs in case of street noise, howler monkeys, for catching a quiet nap on planes and trains, for tuning out the clamor of a busy coffee shop where you're working, or if you have a roommate/partner who likes to watch Netflix while you're trying to sleep.

Swiss Army Knife – I don't go anywhere without mine. You have no idea how many showers, electrical sockets, and doors I've fixed using it! Plus, you never know when you might need a knife (or a bottle opener). Be the kind of girl who carries a Swiss Army Knife. FYI, you'll probably need to pack this in checked baggage for flights, as anything that looks like a weapon isn't allowed in your carryon.

Bamboo cutlery and copper/bamboo straw – I'll say it again. Less plastic will save the planet! Single-use plastic is being banned in many countries (yay!). So, do yourself a favor and get ahead of the game with a bamboo cutlery set, and a copper straw for your mojitos.

Ziplock bags – They come in handy for everything from storing food to protecting your toiletries from leakage. Wash and reuse them.

Electrical adapters – Depending on the country you're visiting, you'll encounter different kinds of electrical outlets. To plug in everything from your cell phone and laptop to your hairdryer, you'll need a travel adapter. I recommend getting one with multiple outlets (so you can power more than one item at a time) and different kinds of outlets for different regions of the world. This isn't the same thing as an electrical converter, which converts 120V to 220V or vice versa. The only time you'll need an international converter is if you're traveling with a device that is not dual voltage.

First aid kit – Make sure it's stocked with band aids, mini-scissors, a small elastic bandage, wound-closure strips, anti-inflammatory/pain reliever, anti-diarrhea tablets, constipation relief, and rehydration sachets. I also carry activated charcoal because it does wonders when I eat something I shouldn't have or have overindulged on alcohol.

Personal care items:
- insect repellent
- wet wipes (many bathrooms don't have toilet paper, and in some countries you can't flush toilet paper.)
- tissues
- hand sanitizer
- paper soap sheets (many bathrooms don't have soap. Just add water and rub your hands to turn these little sheets into foamy hand soap.)
- your preferred menstrual care product (If you're not picky about this, you can find something wherever you go.)

Keep in mind that you can find and purchase most of the personal care products you'll need wherever you travel. You probably won't find the brands you're used to back home, but you'll survive and may discover a new product you like even more. Trying to bring with you every ounce of moisturizer and shampoo that you'll need will take up too much room in your bag. I personally travel with nothing more than a bar of soap and a shampoo bar, as far as toiletries are concerned. As soon as I arrive someplace new, I buy what I need for my stay.

ACCESSORIES

Hat – Depending on how stylish you're feeling, pack a black baseball cap to keep the sun out of your eyes and off your face, or bring something more fashionable, if you have the space in your bag.

Sunglasses – Ensure you're getting UV protection, even if you buy a cheap pair. I travel with a nice (expensive) pair for walking around the city and a cheaper pair for the beach.

Sarong – I have two, and I use them all the time. Sure, they're great as cover-ups; but they're also perfect to replace your towel because you can wear one to the beach then lay on it. I even tuck my sarongs under the top bunk bed to give myself some privacy while sleeping in dorm rooms. You will be amazed at how useful they can be when traveling.

CLOTHING

Mix and match – This is rule number one. Don't pack any single-wear items. Every clothing item you pack should fit you well and go with many other pieces in your bag. I normally include only one patterned top and one patterned bottoms, so every solid-colored piece will go with them. If you pack lots of patterned tops and bottoms, you're going to be limited in what you can wear together. Before packing, lay out everything and do a practice mix and match just to make sure everything goes well together.

Easy wash and quick dry – Pack things that wash easily (leave the dry clean only pieces at home), don't need ironing, are lightweight, and will dry quickly. Avoid bringing anything heavy, as it will take up space. I pack thin, lightweight clothing so I can squeeze in a few more pieces, rather than bringing larger, heavier materials that takes up space. If you're going someplace cold, wear multiple thin layers and invest in a lightweight, wind- and water-resistant jacket that's designed for cold temperatures and folds up nicely.

Buying clothes on the road – I have a one in, one out rule. That means if I buy a new piece of clothing, I have to leave one behind (I donate it or give it away, if it's in decent shape). I do this because I know I don't have extra room in my bag, and I don't have extra money to spend. It helps me to think seriously before buying anything new. That said, you will get fed up of wearing the same outfits over and over, and you'll realize that you're carrying some things around that you rarely wear. So, you'll probably find yourself clothes shopping while you're traveling.

This is generally what I travel with:

8 light tops/vests/t-shirts
3 pairs of shorts (I pack a pair of denim shorts, even though they're heavy)
2 dresses
1 pair of black leggings
1 pair of light trousers
1 pair of jeans
fleece pullover
raincoat
8 panties
2 bra tops
3 bikini tops
2 bikini bottoms
3 pairs of socks
1 belt
2 yoga pants
2 yoga tops

VIRTUAL OFFICE

- laptop
- noise-canceling headphones with a mic
- smartphone
- various chargers
- electrical outlet adapters
- anything else you need for your job

I know another digital nomad who travels with a folding, lightweight standup desk that she puts on top of tables and desks to elevate her laptop. To make that work, she also carries a Bluetooth keyboard and mouse. So, it's possible to take your office with you, regardless of your needs.

OTHER IMPORTANT ITEMS

Photocopies of your passport – I have photos of my passport saved on all of my devices, and I keep a photocopy of it in each of my bags. You never know when you will be asked for this. Plus, if you lose your passport while traveling, having a photocopy makes it much easier to get a replacement.

A fake wallet – I carry a decoy wallet with some expired bank cards (with inactive account numbers) and a small amount of money in case I'm ever robbed or being pickpocketed. I keep some cash and my active credit card in a separate wallet buried deep inside my day bag, preferably in a hidden compartment. When possible, I leave my bank card, more cash, and a back-up credit card safely locked in my accommodations.

Proof of vaccines – This is one you may overlook, but it is important. Before you leave home, get up to date on all of those jabs. Some countries require upon entry (or strongly recommend for your health) proof of certain vaccinations. Ask your doctor's office or health clinic to print confirmation for each vaccination you've received. Keep this in a safe place with your passport.

If you want to know exactly what I pack you can view my full list of recommendations on my blog
clairesitchyfeet.com/resources/digital-nomad-resources/

Chapter 9 - Traveling Solo

Let's get this out of the way right now. Solo travel isn't for everyone. But I truly believe every woman should go on a solo trip once in her life. If you've never traveled solo before but you're seriously thinking about becoming a digital nomad without a fellow travel buddy or a group, my advice is to test the water first. To jump in at the deep end is a lot to deal with emotionally.

Before embarking on my DN life, I had already traveled internationally for work on my own, and I'd been on a mini-holiday by myself. I was no stranger to the long-haul flight. But, I had never backpacked before. My previous experiences traveling by myself were well-organized vacations and work trips.

So, before I fully committed to becoming a solo female digital nomad, I booked a three-week backpacking trip to Thailand with a friend. If you want to cut your teeth as a traveler, Thailand is the place to do it. It's dramatically different than the Western world, it's cheap and safe, and routes have been well-established by the hordes of backpackers who've been going there for decades.

My first trip out of my home country with just a backpack, my guidebooks, and my trusty Pinterest boards was so much fun and a success! After that, I knew beyond a shadow of a doubt I was making the right choice to become a fulltime traveler. Even though I didn't go solo that time, I knew I would have been okay by myself because I had traveled alone before.

Since then, every time I have a meltdown or crisis of confidence, I think back to Thailand and tell myself — say it with me — YOU FUCKING GOT THIS.

What Kind of Traveler Are You?

Once you go solo, it's really difficult to go back to traveling with other people again. Believe me, I have tried.

I've learned that I'm a solo adventurer. My every move is by the skin of my teeth. I hate laying around all day (unless it's on a beach with a frosty cocktail). I want to be up and out the door early to make the most of my days off. When I'm not on an adventure, I'm working. I prefer to work a few 12-hour days, then take a few days off. But not all digital nomads live like this, so I prefer to do my own thing. I make my own schedule and do what I want, when I want.

I'm not saying that I never travel with others or that I don't enjoy some company while I'm traveling. Being a solo adventurer doesn't mean I'm always alone. I just prefer meeting up and hanging out with other solo travelers who are on their own adventures. We have this unspoken rule that we each do what we want to do without a sense of obligation to others' plans. Solo travelers don't get offended when we have different priorities and go our separate ways for the rest of the day (or month). I can't even tell you how refreshing it is to find and share experiences with like-minded travelers, but not feel committed to make all of our decisions together and spend every day together.

When a fellow solo traveler bails on me at the last moment because another adventure caught their eye or they suddenly have work to do, it's like, "Sure, no worries. See you later." We understand that we're all on our own journey. Sometimes our paths will cross, and it will be magic. Other times, we do our own thing—and guess what—it's still magic.

I love the spontaneity and freedom of solo travel. And I especially love the crazy nights with random strangers who become lifelong friends and travel companions. But, after three days of constantly being in another traveler's company, I want to lock myself in the bathroom to get some space.

You may feel entirely different about travel. You may crave the companionship, ongoing conversation, and deep connection that can happen when you share your travel adventure with someone else.

If you've never before taken a trip by yourself, my advice is to give it a try before you fully commit to the solo travel life. Before you quit your job, pack up your life, and hop on a plane to Timbuktu, take a solo road trip around your own country. Or, spend a week in another country where they speak your language, so it feels like a stepping stone. Or, jump right in with a short vacation in Chiang Mai, Thailand, where you'll find plenty of solo female travelers from around the world. This experience will either completely thrill you or reveal that solo travel isn't your bag. Either way it is better to know in advance if you prefer solo to traveling with companions.

If solo travel isn't for you, and you don't have a free-agent friend or partner who can join you, you do have other options. There are digital nomad travel groups, co-living DN homes, female-only travel tour companies, and working/networking retreats you can join to ensure you'll have some company and support from the moment you depart. Many of these organizations even handle some of the planning and logistics for you (at a premium cost, of course).

Chapter 10 - Safety

Worried about your safety when traveling solo? You aren't alone. This is one of the top concerns for most women before they start traveling. Even if you're a seasoned traveler, safety is likely to be a concern for you, your family, and your friends. I can't even tell you how many times I'm asked, "Is it safe there?" My answer is always the same. Where is it 100% safe to be a woman?

The sad reality is you are more likely to be attacked by a man you know in your own home than you are by a stranger while traveling. In the three years I have been traveling fulltime, I have yet to run into any physical danger. That's not to say I haven't found myself in some sticky situations. In some cases, I should have known better. Other times, I was just very lucky things didn't go terribly wrong. I have been robbed twice, and both instances were non-confrontational. The first time, I was pickpocketed. The second time, some guy attempted to steal my daypack. I chased after him and got it back. That was a very bad idea. Don't do that, if you're ever in a similar situation.

In this chapter, I address some common safety issues you may be concerned about, and I share a few ways you can reduce your risks while traveling.

Research: Because Knowledge Is Power

If you're traveling somewhere new to you, do some serious research. Look at the crime statistics and, specifically, the number of assaults on women. The idea isn't to scare you; it's to empower you. If you compare these stats to those in cities you've lived in and visited before, you will likely be surprised by what you find.

When I did this, I learned that my hometown wasn't much different from most of the places I was traveling to. In many cases, the crime rates were actually lower outside of my hometown. Crime happens EVERYWHERE, so put it into context. Being armed with these stats will also help as rebuttals when your family and friends voice concerns for your safety.

Make sure to research the neighborhoods where you're staying. Check reviews on booking.com, Airbnb, Hostel world, and TripAdvisor. Focus on feedback about safety concerns like door locks and broken windows. After your stay, please leave reviews and be honest about any safety concerns you had. If you don't share your negative experiences, then other women will never know. We need to have each other's backs when traveling, and this includes in our reviews.

Sign up for government safety warnings from the UK and the US. I've found that the UK is a bit less fear-mongering. Check out the local newspaper online (if they have one) so you can read about any local issues.

Emergency Numbers

Before you arrive in a new place, identify the emergency phone numbers for that country or locality, including the embassy for your country. Dig a little deeper if you're travelling to a country known to have issues with the police or government. Sometimes it's better to go directly to your embassy or tourist-specific police.

Booking Your Accommodations

While I've already shared how I go about finding and booking accommodations, I want to emphasize that reserving your first night or two in a hotel or hostel in a decent area can make your arrival to a new place safer and less scary. There is nothing more stressful than pounding the pavement with your backpack or suitcase looking for a good place to rest your tired bones. It can make you appear a bit lost and vulnerable to someone looking to take advantage of your situation.

Before you leave your current location, save the following information on your phone and write it down on paper in case your phone dies or is lost/stolen:

- Full name and address of your accommodations
  If it's an Airbnb home, I also recommend looking closely on Google Maps and writing down the name of a nearby landmark like a hotel or restaurant as a reference point because small residences can be hard to find. It's not a bad idea to look at Google Maps' street view and take a screenshot of the outside of the building so you can recognize it. I once had to get escorted by the police to my Airbnb in Bogota as I was in tears after an hour of searching.

- Phone number of the accommodations
  This comes in handy if you or your taxi driver need to call them because you can't find the place, or if you arrive there and no one answers the door.

- Name of your host (if it's an Airbnb)

Public Transportation Safety Tips

Make sure you know how to get from the airport or train/bus station to your accommodations. It's not only stressful to figure this out when you arrive at your destination tired, hangry, and carrying all of your bags. Doing so can also make you look like a target to those seeking to take advantage of women in that situation.

If public transport (metro/subway, bus, train, or airport transfer van) is easy and I'm on my own, I always use it. If I'm travelling with others or it's difficult to get to my destination using public transport, I get a taxi or an Uber.

Before you travel, figure out the following. Keep this information saved on your phone and written down in case your phone dies or goes missing:

- Which train, metro, or bus you need to get on
- Where you need to go to wait for the train, bus, or taxi
- How much this transportation costs (especially if you're using a taxi, so you can avoid an argument with the driver)

Always take a licensed taxi. When you get in the car, take a photo of the taxi registration or license. If you can be sneaky, take a pic of the driver, too.

Store all of your important (and expensive) things on you and in the daypack or purse you're going to keep on your lap when you're in a taxi or on a bus.

Once you settle in, you'll likely use public transportation and taxis/Ubers during your stay. As part of your research, determine how safe it is for women to take taxis, especially at night. You'll also want to know if walking at night (even in pairs/groups) is considered safe. This varies drastically from place to place. For example, in many South American countries, it's not advisable for a woman to take a taxi at night alone. But in Europe, it's considered pretty safe. In many cities, public transport is very safe during the day, but at night, it can be very different.

Avoid travelling alone at night if you can help it.

Using Google Maps for Safety

I don't even know what I did before this app. Make sure you have it on your phone before you even leave home. I use it for turn-by-turn walking/biking directions, information about which buses or metro lines to take to which stops, and to predict how long it should take my taxi or Uber to reach my destination. Did you know you can also use this app offline? Simply go to your settings, select "offline areas," and download maps for your area. A good alternative to Google Maps is Maps Me, which works offline in countries where you don't have a phone signal, like Cuba.

But, if you're walking down the road staring at your phone, you aren't taking in your surroundings, and you're making yourself appear unsure of where you are. To prevent looking like a target, put your headphones on and your phone in your purse, fanny pack, or backpack. If you need to take a look at the map, stop someplace that looks safe and well lit.

Pin Dropping

ALWAYS let someone know where you are. If you're going somewhere new, like on a Tinder date, to a large event by yourself, or to a part of town that doesn't have the best reputation, let someone you trust know exactly where you're going and who you will be with, as well as what time you intend to be home.

I do this by dropping a pin at my location on Google Maps, but you can use whatever map app you prefer, and I text it to a few of my good travel friends. A lot of my social media is automated, so I also check in with family regularly, letting them know I'm okay because my online presence doesn't necessarily mean I've been online recently.

There is also an app called bSafe which will let you set up a network of your chosen people to share your location with. It has a "follow me" option in which your family and friends can follow your GPS signal as you make your way home in real time. It will even trigger an alert if you haven't checked in after a certain length of time.

Safety Items

These items won't take up much room in your bag and can help you feel a bit safer.

A door wedge – I got this tip from a fellow solo traveler who worked in the hotel industry. If you're feeling a bit unsafe in your hostel or hotel room, push this under your door to wedge it shut from the inside. What a brilliant idea!

A whistle – It's light and loud. I keep one in my bag in case of emergency. You might be surprised how a loud noise can get you out of a sticky situation and call the attention of those around you.

Important Documents

I recommend traveling with at least two printed photocopies of your passport and any other essential documents. Save a scan of your driver's license, passport, and proof of your vaccinations in the cloud and on your phone. I also email images of these documents to someone I trust (like my parents). Keep a photocopy of your passport in each bag. Keep your actual passport in a different bag when traveling, and store it in a lockbox, if your accommodations has one.

Money and Credit Cards

When carrying cash, divide it up amongst your bags and pockets in each bag. I also carry two wallets—a real one and a fake. The fake one holds a little cash and a few deactivated credit/bank cards. If I'm robbed, I can just hand over the fake. If my real wallet gets stolen, I won't lose everything.

If your credit or debit card is lost or stolen, you'll need to call to cancel the card immediately, so, write down and save on your phone (in the cloud or in a locked folder) the account number and customer service phone number for each of your cards.

Utilizing Facebook Groups for Safety

The internet can be a pretty terrifying place. But, in spite of all of the fake news, graphic content, trigger warnings, and internet trolls, the web can enable you to feel safer as you roam the world. It's no coincidence that the number of solo female travelers has recently grown tremendously, in part because of the internet's resources and its ability to connect us through social media and GPS-based apps. I've already advised you (begged you?) to join the many Facebook groups and other digital nomad online networks out there. Your safety is yet another reason why you should do this.

Once you've already read the official government warnings and the local news, you may also want to hear some personal stories from other solo female travelers. There's a lot of chat in online forums and Facebook groups about unsafe areas even though the media is not reporting it. In these Facebook groups, you can search for relevant conversation threads or post your own question for the members who live in or have visited that area.

Let's say you're traveling with a friend or hanging out with another solo female traveler, and you suddenly can't get ahold of them on their phone. And they're not answering their door. Aside from contacting local police, you can also post their photo and description on the local digital nomad Facebook group. The same Facebook groups can be helpful if you have an accident and need help. A number of missing people and SOS calls shared within these groups have inspired members to jump into action! I remember a girl in Israel put out an SOS on Facebook, and within an hour, another girl had come to her aid and got her out of a bad situation. They posted a selfie the next day at the Dead Sea having a great time. There are tens of thousands of members in some of these groups, so there's almost always someone nearby who can respond to your SOS.

Here are some of my favorite Facebook travel groups (that aren't location-specific):

Solo Travel Advice - mixed-gender solo travel group run by a good friend of mine (Stephanie)
Girls Gone Global - run by Aylne from Dear Alyne
The Solo Female Traveler Network
Solo Women Travel Tribe
Go Wonder

And if you happen to be traveling in Latin America join my group Solo Female Travelers Latin America.

Watch Your Drinks

As a rule, you should be very careful with alcohol abroad. In certain places, it's common for men to spike women's drinks, so do your research about which neighborhoods and which bars you visit for a night out. Avoid leaving your drink unattended on a table or at the bar.

I'm in my late 30's now, so partying isn't high on my agenda most of the time. I prefer a few beers and an early night. When I drink, I tend to go out early and don't stay out very late, unless I'm in a safe area. I rarely get drunk while I'm traveling because alcohol can cloud my judgment and make me more vulnerable. When I do let my hair down and party, I make sure I'm 100% comfortable in my environment and trust the people I'm with.

One of the issues I have personally found when going out with new friends I've met while traveling is that they can be totally different people when they have a few drinks. It's worth having a chat before you go out to talk through what to do in case you lose each other or if one of you decides to go home with someone they met that night. How will you get home if that happens? Talking about these things before you go out helps you put a safety plan in place so you know how to handle the situation if it comes up.

I know it's sad to have to worry so much about these things. And, even if you're careful and drink only fizzy water, something bad can happen. To say that a victimized woman should have done more to protect herself is victim blaming. But, being cautious about alcohol and your environment can help you reduce your risk and feel safer.

Insurance

The reality is, things can go wrong at any moment. If you get sick or are in an accident, your medical bills could skyrocket. Something could happen to your devices, such as your laptop. As a long-term traveler, you need to be as prepared as possible. One of the best ways to do this is to get insurance before you leave.

For the first year I traveled, I used World Nomads backpacker's insurance, and this was the best deal for me. They cover several things, such as lost luggage, pregnancy, accidents, dental care, stolen items, natural disasters, and much more. Although they are a great company, my coverage was expensive, and a lot of their benefits aren't worth it for me anymore.

I now use Safetywing Digital Nomad insurance for medical expenses. Their coverage includes mopeds, scuba diving, and other things that I need. The policy automatically extends each month, unless I cancel it. I choose not to insure my computer equipment anymore. I'm just very careful, and I have enough savings in my bank account to replace things.

I've written an in-depth article on my blog about this topic, so please check it out for more information about travel insurance.

clairesitchyfeet.com/long-term-travel-insurance/

Trust Your Intuition

You know that feeling you get that something isn't quite right or something bad is going to happen? Well, trust it. If you feel at all uncomfortable about something, some place, or some person, then listen to your instincts and get outta there. Simple.

Solo travel can be tremendously empowering and liberating, but it can also make you feel pretty vulnerable at times. That said, I often felt just as vulnerable in my home country as I do in a foreign place. So, I never let fear stop me from doing something. Speaking of which …

Chapter 11 - Dealing with Fear

You know the number one enemy of any badass solo female traveler?

Fear. For real.

When I tell people what I do and about the places I've traveled solo, nine times out of ten I get some variation of "Aren't you afraid? I'd be too scared."

The truth is, I'm scared a lot.

I was scared when I lived in the UK. I'm scared when I visit my mum in the U.S. I'm scared at least 10 times a day. Since I can remember, I have been afraid of men. Not all men (obviously), but pretty much all men I don't know. I know it may not be logical, but it's how I feel. If you think I am a crazy woman for saying this then I urge you to read some articles by Caitlin Moran, who explains it better than I ever could.

The #MeToo movement put a spotlight on the issues all women face, to some degree. I know it's #notallmen but it is #allwomen. Statistically, as a woman, you are more likely to be abused, raped, or murdered by a man you know than a stranger. In fact, all of my friends who have been raped or abused by men (and sadly there are many) have known their assailant.

As Margaret Atwood famously said, "Men are afraid that women will laugh at them. Women are afraid that men will kill them."

So, it's not that I'm afraid of solo travel, I'm just afraid in general.

Think about it.

Does that mean I'm going to lock myself away and never talk to another man again for fear of being attacked? No, of course not. My logical brain knows that not every man wants to attack me, and that most men are good humans who are kind to their mothers and sisters and other humans. So, with the same logic, I go gallivanting around the world on my own because I'm not going to let fear stop me.

The way I see it, you have two choices: sit around and live in fear, or live the life you want and be brave AF.

I choose to be brave. I refuse to live in fear.

I'm also not reckless and careless. I rarely drink while I'm traveling because I just don't feel safe doing so (I even wrote about this for the Huffington post). I always carry a knife and a whistle. I do a thorough safety check of any new place I'm traveling to and follow the advice I get. All of these things help me feel more in control and less fearful.

To most, I probably don't come across as a fearful person.

I'm the kind of person who is calm in a crisis. Maybe like me, you can be strong for others around you, then have a bit of a breakdown when you're alone. Spiders don't bother me, and I don't think twice about swimming in open waters. But my fear of flying and heights once drove me to despair.

For as long as I can remember, I have been terrified of flying. Plus, I had a crippling fear of heights. Add to that, I get sporadic spells of depression and deal with constant anxiety about pretty much anything and everything. So, I'm no stranger to managing fear. My rational brain knew that my fear of heights was silly. But it wasn't just in my head, this fear took over my entire body. On planes, I felt every tremor like needles sticking into me. Walking over a bridge or down stairs I could see through was enough to make me a shaky, sweaty mess.

Although this fear never stopped me from flying, it was exhausting and terrifying, especially as I prepared for a life of constant travel. Before most flights, I would take a Valium (or two) or wash down sleeping pills with some alcohol to send me into a travel coma. But the heights thing constantly held me back from doing and seeing things I wanted to experience.

I can't say for sure the moment the fear left my body. But, letting go of so many material *things* while preparing for my life as a digital nomad helped me let go of this heavy fear. I had been physically and emotionally holding on to so many things for way too long. In this process of letting go, I started to let the light back in.

This quote (which may or may not have come from Buddha) resonated with me and helped me through this period. "In the end, only three things matter: how much you loved, how gently you lived, and how gracefully you let go of things not meant for you."

Letting go of things and fears can be excruciating, but also liberating. You might just end up feeling lighter and less afraid.

When I started my journey, a good friend, Hayley, accompanied me. Hayley is a qualified Rolfer (a practitioner of an alternative medicine body-realignment technique called Rolfing). We've been on quite an emotional journey over the years of our friendship, even though we are often absent from each other's lives for months on end then come back together, often during transitional times in each other's lives. We've been through broken bones, leftover trauma, job loss, home loss, grief, and joy.

Hayley offered to do some Rolfing sessions on me with a focus on releasing fear trapped in my body. At least I think that's how it works! I'd had Rolfing before for a physical injury, and I swear by it, as many dancers do. But I must admit, I wasn't convinced Rolfing would release me from my fears.

After Hayley left, I didn't think too much about the treatment. Until I got on a plane from NYC to Miami, the first of two flights. I was apprehensive, but not quite as terrified as I normally was. The second flight that day took me from Miami to Guatemala. I felt completely different. I was less stressed during takeoff, and as we approached the landing, I looked out the window at this beautiful country scattered with lakes and volcanos. An incredible calm came over me, and I felt completely at peace. I actually began to cry.

Then I started noticing small things. Like I was able to lean over a balcony or stand close to the edge without getting the shakes. I didn't break into a sweat while on a bus speeding around switchbacks on a mountain (well no more than any sane person does as a passenger on a Guatemalan chicken bus).

When I was hiking up to a mirador (lookout point) in Guatemala, I realized something had truly changed in me. At this point, I was halfway up some crazy wooden stairs on the side of a mountain. And I thought, "Holy crap, I'm not afraid." In truth, I'm not sure why I'm no longer afraid of heights or flying. Becoming a solo traveler forced me to let go physically and mentally of so many things that once made me feel trapped and afraid to move.

Of course, solo travel isn't going to make you fearless. But when you change your life so drastically — and you survive — you can put your fears into perspective and loosen your grip on the ones that hold you back.

Chapter 12 - Finding Your Community

Want to know the secret to feeling less on your own as a solo traveler? Find your community. No one else in your life is going to understand the ups and downs of this nomadic lifestyle quite like other digital nomads.

After three years of traveling, I have a solid circle of badass women (and a few incredible men) in my life. They have become my support network through the ups and downs of being a nomad.

Where can you find your community?

On Facebook, Instagram, Nomad List, Meetup, and Couch Surfing. There's also digital nomad-friendly social and networking gatherings, meetups, workshops, retreats, conferences, and co-working/co-living spaces like Nomad Cruise and Nomad House. You can find all of these on social media. Sometimes, you'll meet and connect with another traveler while working in a café, hanging out in a hostel, or at a local yoga class.

Most of the digital nomad Facebook groups I belong to are all-female groups. I have found these groups to be far more supportive and nurturing than mixed-gender groups. I rarely post in the mixed groups because, in general, they're a lot more negative and there's way too much mansplaining for my liking.

My favorite groups are the various Digital Nomad Girls groups on Facebook. They are small, well managed, and super supportive. The larger groups filled with solo female travelers can get a little confrontational at times, but one thing I love about them is how safe they made me feel when I first started traveling.

I also met several good friends in these groups, many of whom I have never met in person. I call them 'good friends' because that's the level to which we support each other. The fact that we have never met in real life makes no difference. One friend I connected with based on a post where she mentioned living close to where I was living. So, after an exchange of messages, I added her on Facebook with the intention to meet in real life. But life happened, and that meeting never took place. However, over the course of the last few years, we have emotionally supported each other through some pretty crazy times.

When I was living in Medellín, Colombia, I added a woman on Facebook from a local DN group in the hope of going salsa dancing together. That never happened, but we remained virtual friends long after I left. She saw on social that I was living in Playa del Carmen, Mexico, and she virtually introduced me to a well-known travel vlogger who was also in Playa. We ended up doing a collaboration, and she inspired me to start vlogging.

The woman who introduced us eventually came to Playa, and we got to hang out in real life and go salsa dancing together. She introduced me to another British woman who became one of my best friends, although we have met only once or twice in real life. She's the person in my life who I tell what I had for breakfast and we are now co-directors of a Digital Marketing Agency along with another Nomad I met through Facebook and whom neither of us have physically met in real life.

I met another one of my best friends and long-term collaborators via Instagram. She reached out to me after a guy she was dating told her I was living in Playa del Carmen. We met there and have been friends ever since.

I have a million stories like this of interesting people I've connected with online.

I'm grateful for all of them, and they are my community.

Dealing with all the Goodbyes

Friends are going to come and go in your life, even if you never move to a new place, but when you become part of the nomad community, you have to say goodbye more often. Often, your new travel bestie packs their bags and heads off to their next destination. Other times, you're the one who has to leave behind a place and people you've come to love.

I cried for a week before I left Guatemala, I cried all the way to the airport when I left Colombia, and I will probably sob for a month when I move on from Mexico. No one understands this like my digital nomad friends. My friends from back home would just tell me to stay, while my nomad friends understand that I can't.

There's a very strong possibility that I will meet up with my nomad friends again. I'm heading to Las Vegas soon to meet up with a woman with whom I shared a hostel room in Cuba. You'll be surprised how many times you'll run into (or plan to reunite with) the same digital nomads in new places. While traveling solo, you will have the most interesting network of acquaintances and group of close friends who live and work all over the word. That means you're likely to have your own personal tour guide when you visit them.

Networking

An unexpected benefit of building your circle is it will help you find work. I don't generally have to apply for jobs anymore because most of my work comes from my nomad friends referring clients to me. This relationship works both ways, as I'm always recommending members of my circle to those seeking professionals with their skills.

Sometimes, you'll meet other nomads who can help you develop an aspect of your work, like improving your website design or copy. You might meet someone who can teach you a few things about digital marketing, public speaking, or photography. Maybe you have a skillset that they need help with. Establishing your community can lead to mutually beneficial professional collaborations and partnerships.

Overcoming Loneliness

It's going to take you some time to build your community. Even once you have people in your virtual life, they aren't much good if you want someone to physically hang out with. Despite what you may think, I have always found it much easier to meet people when I'm traveling solo than when traveling with others.

Beyond all the social media and app-based means of meeting new people, I look for fun things to do where I can meet others with similar interests.

It depends on what you're into, but here are some activities I've participated in around the world that lend themselves to socializing:

CrossFit — Yes, I know it's a bit of a cult and people get obsessed with it. I'll hold up my hands because I was one of them. But, I could walk into any CrossFit box around the world and be greeted with a warm smile and the offer of friendship.

Yoga — Some of the most incredible people I've met along my travels have been in a yoga studio. When I first arrived in Guatemala, I was having a horrible time. Then I took a yoga class with the most wonderful human. I knew instantly we would be friends, and this was a real turning point for me. I met most of my friends in Guatemala through this yoga instructor. I even become a yoga teacher and worked in her yoga studio while I lived there.

Scuba Diving — One thing I love about scuba diving is that it doesn't attract just one type of person. Out of any other sport/activity I've engaged with, diving attracts very diverse groups of people. I have met so many amazing people through diving who I never would have met in a million years if it wasn't for our mutual love of the ocean.

Dancing — I took up salsa dancing when I lived in Colombia, and it completely changed my social life. Going out at night alone has always been a sticking point for me. I will happily go out to eat by myself, but going out drinking alone just never interested me. Then I learned to dance salsa! Now, the first thing I do when I get to a new place is find the best salsa dancing spot. I've met a lot of awesome people through dance. Even if I don't know anyone, I feel totally confident going out alone to dance the night away.

Maybe you're more interested in cooking classes, art workshops, jamming with other musicians, learning a new language, playing soccer, or hiking. Think of the activities you enjoy at home with your friends, and when you're by yourself. Or, maybe there's a new hobby you've been meaning to try. With a little research online and social media, you can find a local group activity that sparks your interest. Group activities accelerate the friendship-building process. You have a shared interest that brings you together and gives you something to focus on and talk about. It makes it really easy to build on that foundation.

Chapter 13 - Working On The Road

Newsflash. You are not, I repeat, NOT a backpacker.

I sometimes refer to myself as a backpacker because I travel with a backpack. But backpackers don't work unless they run out of money. Even then, they often just do a bit of under-the-table work so they can buy more beer. That isn't me, and it won't be you either.

If you're staying in hostels and hanging out with backpackers, then there is going to come a time when you have to say "no" to them because you need to work. I didn't realize I wasn't a backpacker until I was slightly stoned and drinking a beer IN MY BED at 2pm on a Wednesday. For the third day in a row. It was just as I was about to have a nap that I realized I wasn't a backpacker. My backpacking friends could spend all day every day drinking and smoking weed. But I was a digital nomad. I had to work at least 20 hours a week to break even. So, from then on, I acknowledged that my lifestyle was different. I started spending less time with backpackers and more time with other DNs.

Time Management

As digital nomads, we have to strike a healthy, functional balance with work and play.

The great thing about determining your own schedule is that you can work when you are most productive. I prefer to work in the mornings and a little in the evening, Monday through Friday. I go out and do fun things in the afternoons or evenings when I can. And I take weekends off. If I'm preparing to go off the grid for a few weeks, I'll most likely do a full week of crazy hours to schedule my blog posts and ensure all of my freelance work is done.

If you're a night owl, hit the beach (or go for a walk, to the market, or the gym) in late-morning, then work throughout the afternoon/evening until it's time to meet up with your new friends for dinner. I've met DNs who choose to work late at night because that's when their brains are ready to hustle or because they're working New York work hours from a bungalow in South East Asia.

Where to Work

Hostels — Many hostels have an open, shared space where you can work, especially the international hostel chains (like Selina), which are designed with DNs in mind. I value the social aspect of hostels more than I need total privacy for work.

Coworking Spaces — I like to find a coworking space where I can work part-time (twice a week for five hours a day). Being in a shared space with other remote workers can help keep you motivated. Plus, coworking spaces are designed with work in mind, so they often offer perks like a copier and fax machine, mail services, free coffee, quiet spaces for making phone calls, and various seating/desk options.

Here are the best resources for finding local coworking spaces worldwide: www.coworker.com, www.copass.org, and www.getcroissant.com. Most coworking spaces offer free day passes so you can try them out first. If there are a number of coworking spaces to choose from, you can give each of them a try to find your best fit.

Coffee Shops—Good Wi-Fi is hit or miss in coffee shops and restaurants, but the local digital nomad Facebook group or Nomad List Slack chat can tell you which cafés have reliable Wi-Fi, plenty of electrical outlets, and the best avocado toast.

Your Home—If you need complete peace and quiet to get your work done (or if you work late hours), you may prefer to work from your hotel room or Airbnb. If you live with other digital nomads, you can turn your living and dining room into a coworking space and encourage each other to stay in the flow.

Beach or Poolside—I've been known to take my laptop to the beach on occasion, in classic DN-style, but in reality, it's more challenging to work in the sun. It's hot, the sand gets everywhere, you can't see beyond the glare on your screen, and everyone else is enjoying the place with a beer instead of a looming deadline.

It's all trial and error until you find which work environments work best for you.

Chapter 14 - Volunteering

Want to know my secret to heading off to be a digital nomad with $1,000 in savings and not quite enough income to survive each month? Workaway or Workpackers.

Both programs places nomads in volunteer positions around the world. Nomadic volunteers help local families, organizations, farms, ranches, schools, and other populations by volunteering their time and skills, based on the hosts' needs. In exchange, the volunteers typically get free accommodations, some meals, and invaluable human and animal connections. You pay a small fee to join both organizations, you're still responsible for your own transportation to get to the destinations, and you'll pay all of your other expenses.

Workaway or Workpackers could be a great fit for you, if you have the need. If you already have a lot of paid work to do while you travel and can afford to cover your expenses, then don't even consider this option. It's not a good match for a fulltime work schedule.

There are other platforms that offer a similar service, but these are the best known. You could also contact companies directly to ask them about their volunteering/work-exchange programs.

My Workaway Experience

I did work-exchange for a tour company in Guatemala. I managed the company's social media and helped out in their hostel. The work was fun, and it fit around my paid work. I had a roof over my head, a pretty good breakfast each morning, and opportunities to hike volcanos with the group. I also got discounted Spanish lessons and met some incredible people. I was supposed to stay for two weeks, but ended up there for two months.

I traveled in Guatemala for eight months, and my total accommodations bill came to less than $100 (for nights in a hostel between Workways). In one month, I spent only $315 on living expenses. This enabled me to save $200-$500 a month. It was a lifesaver at the time.

As an added bonus, I learned so much about social media management, which helped me attract paid work in that field. I also learned a lot about the tour industry, which helped me as a blogger when pitching to companies. When my writing eventually started paying off, and more paid work was coming my way, I no longer needed to volunteer in order to pay the rent. The experience was a great buffer to get me through that transitional period and the first part of my journey. But after nine months, I had found my footing, both logistically and financially. I have this experience to thank for several of the jobs I'm currently doing.

How Does It Work?

Each volunteer arrangement is slightly different, but most offer accommodations and food in exchange for around 20 to 25 hours of work each week. The jobs vary greatly from web development and photography to teaching yoga and helping care for farm animals. You can search by location and job preference, and apply through the platform.

The normal working day is four to five hours a day. Double check how many days of the week the host needs help. Some expect the volunteer to work seven days a week, and I would avoid those positions. That said, if there are four volunteers and only one of you needs to be there at any given time, then you are generally left to work it out amongst yourselves. The hosts don't mind, as long as the work gets done.

Workaway and Workpacker conditions vary drastically. I stayed in some pretty awful places with easy work and lovely people. I also stayed in some nice places with not-so-nice people and really challenging work. My first Workaway had no Wi-Fi in our accommodations, and there were three of us sharing a very small room. If you need good Wi-Fi and prefer your own room, your Workaway options will be limited. Don't trust what the profile/job description says. Email them to ask about the accommodations and anything else that you can't live or work without.

Why You Should Consider using Workaway or Workpacker

- Save money on food and accommodations.
- Meet other travelers.
- Sometimes you earn extra money through tips.
- Meet and work with local people.
- The work is often really interesting.

- Learn new skills on the job.
- It can be a great way to build your CV if you are still figuring out your digital nomad career path.
- Because the work commitment is part-time, you'll have some time to do your freelance work and build your own client base.
- It can be a great option if your funds run low or your regular work dries up a bit.

You can read more about my Workpackers experience on my blog clairesitchyfeet.com/using-workaway-for-travel/

Chapter 15 - Logistics

The most stressful situations I have been in while traveling have all included banking. On more than one occasion, I have cried real tears of pure frustration, spent hours on the phone, and taken to ranting on Twitter.

Here are some shitty situations I found myself in over the past few years.

After hiking a volcano, I was so tired that I forgot my only debit card inside an ATM in Guatemala. While I was heading home in less than a month, I had very little cash left. Guatemala has no postal service; they went on strike a few years ago and it never returned. Receiving money through Western Union is one of the most stressful things I've had to deal with.

On another occasion, my phone was stolen, and I replaced it. I needed to add my banking app to my new phone, but to do this, the app sends a code to my phone. Well, I didn't have a UK cell number anymore, and the app wouldn't let me add my foreign mobile number. After many, many, frustrating phone calls, I ended up having to give the bank my dad's mobile number. Now, before I can do anything with that account, I need to make sure my dad is on hand to forward the access code. He also receives a notification every time my bank account is running low on funds. Super annoying for him and embarrassing for me.

In addition to the stupid mobile code, I needed to get another code from a pin century machine. It's a little thing I put my card into, type in my pin number, and it gives me a code. Simple, right? It would've been easy if the machine hadn't run out of battery a month before.

I have lost count of all the phone calls I've made in attempt to resolve this—with no success. I had to survive without my online banking for almost a year before I was able to get a friend to bring a replacement century machine from the UK.

What have I learned from these experiences?

- Have more than one active bank account.
- Have more than one debit card.
- Have two credit cards, ideally.
- Buy a Skype number, unless you're keeping your phone number from home.
- Get a bank account that doesn't require one of those pin century things (Barclays UK, I'm looking at you).

In an effort to avoid these frustrating situations, my advice is to establish at least two checking accounts before you become a digital nomad. Ensure that each account has its own debit card, and ideally one is a Visa card and one a MasterCard. Ensure that these accounts don't charge fees for every withdrawal from an international ATM or one not affiliated with your bank. Never store or carry these two debit cards in the same place at the same time.

I currently have a British bank account, a U.S. bank account, and a Mexican bank account. I also have PayPal, Stripe, TransferWise, Zelle bank transfer, and a few other online accounts that enable me to send and receive money. While the modern world catches up with the nomadic lifestyle, it's best to keep your options open and diversify the types of banking and money transfer accounts you use. When possible, avoid accounts that require you to have battery-operated pin machines.

In addition to your debit cards, you need two credit cards, if possible. These are for booking flights and accommodations (provides more protection than paying with a debit card) and any emergencies. Again, one Visa card and one MasterCard is best. Some countries accept only Visa (like Cuba), while others prefer MasterCard (like certain places in Russia).

Go Paperless

Once you have all of your accounts set up, streamline everything. Sign up for automatic payments to ensure you're never late on a payment. Sign up for online banking and email delivery for monthly statements and notifications.

It's important to maintain access to your paper mail (snail-mail or post) while you're traveling. This is where you'll receive important notifications that some banks and other organizations, companies, and government agencies won't email to you.

Before I left for my new nomadic life, I spent a lot of time looking for a way to avoid having my family deal with my mail in my absence. Because I no longer have a fixed address and don't intend on returning anytime soon, I needed a cost-effective way to deal with my mail long-term. That's when I discovered postal services that manage your paper mail for a fee.

You have to pay for each piece of physical mail you receive, so it's important that before you do this, you go paperless as much as possible. Go through the notification settings on each of your accounts (banking, credit card, health insurance, etc.) and change all of them to paperless (email and/or text notifications).

Using a postal service

There are several different postal services you can use. I personally use UK Postbox. In the U.S., you can use US Global Mail or EarthClassMail. You sign up for their services by choosing the level of service you want. I initially went with an all-inclusive plan, so I paid a flat fee for the first year. Now I don't receive as much mail, so I pay as I go. Every time a letter is mailed to my post office box, my paid postal service scans the outside of the envelope and emails me the image. It's up to me how I want the postal service to deal with it. The options are open, scan the contents and email to me, forward to another address, shred, or recycle.

It's so simple to use, and it's been a lifesaver for me. The postal service has been able to forward new bank cards and important documents to me wherever I am in the world. And, I didn't have any issues changing my bank account mailing addresses to my P.O. Box address (which I thought I might).

Although it is always an option to ask a family member to deal with your mail, if you're traveling long-term, it's far better to use a postal service. It will take the pressure off your family member and keep you in control of your mail.

Chapter 16 – Technology

Figuring out your technology needs is going to take a little time and planning. I've changed my tech essentials drastically over the past few years. As my freelance work has evolved and grown, so has the amount of equipment I need to have with me.

This is my current list of tech essentials for personal use and work:

- MacBook Air
- Laptop charger
- Laptop case
- Laptop stand (I use a Mofit as it just attaches to the bottom of my laptop so takes up no space)
- Extension cord
- A tablet and its charger
- HDML cable and adapter
- 2 external hard drives
- Noise-canceling headphones with mic
- Wi-Fi Hotspot (I have a Teppy)
- Unlocked smart phone
- Portable power bank/battery charger
- Electrical outlet adapter (converts outlets for European, American, Asian, and other type plugs)
- DSLR camera with 3 lenses
- GoPro with accessories
- Mirrorless camera
- Drone
- Tripod
- Gorilla tripod
- Shotgun mic
- Pin mic

This is a fair number of things to carry around. It's also the reason I now have a carryon suitcase with a very good built-in lock. I put all of my expensive equipment in there and wheel it around, so it doesn't break my back. Also, unless you are planning on blogging or vlogging you probably won't need half of the camera equipment I'm lugging around with me.

What Technology Will You Need as a DN?

Make a list. Think about the things you need for your lifestyle and to do your work full time, long term, which may mean eight (or more) hours a day. Consider ergonomics, battery life for your various devices, and any external gadgets you rely on (like a Bluetooth mouse, speaker, camera, keyboard, smart watch, or fitness tracker). I would strongly recommend making sure you have everything you need before you start traveling, as it can be very expensive to buy technology in many countries.

If you can't get an affordable international calling and data plan on your phone, I would seriously think about investing in an online phone number. I have one with Skype. There's an annual fee for the number, but to make voice and video calls via Skype is very reasonable. I think I added $10 to my Skype account over two years ago, and I still have a few dollars left. I use it primarily for calling my bank and credit card companies.

If you're going to teach online, I strongly recommend getting an external camera because my laptop's built-in camera often failed. You can get a small one, so it doesn't take up too much room.

Think about insuring the more expensive pieces of equipment against breakage, malfunctioning, and theft. Consider what steps you'll need to take to replace/repair these items with or without insurance when you're in another country.

Digital Nomad-Friendly Software, Cloud Storage, and Apps

Click up — This web/mobile app is the only project management tool I've used that actually keeps me on track. It has a google chrome extension that lets me track the time I spend on a task and it has a Slack integration. It's perfect for teams, but just as useful for solo projects. If it's not in Clickup, it doesn't get done.

Slack — Discovering this mobile-friendly communication platform was a game-changer for me. Each of my long-term clients has their own Slack channel where all of our work chats take place. This helps them and me avoid searching through emails to find important conversations.

Google Drive — You need to back up your files and documents in case your laptop gets lost or broken. I keep nothing on my hard drive. Everything is backed up on Google Drive (and on both of my external hard drives).

Google Photos — I consider this to be the perfect cloud backup for all of my photos and videos. As soon as I've edited some pictures, I save them on Google Photos (and on both external hard drives). Ever since I lost a hard drive full of photos, I'm fanatical about saving them in three places.

Google Translate — Did you know you can open the Google Translate mobile app, hold up your phone's camera to a sign or restaurant menu in any language, and it will translate it for you instantly? It's not always a great translation, but it will help you get by.

Adobe's Creative Cloud — If you're going to be editing lots of photos and videos, I recommend paying for the full CC suite of software. For my needs, I haven't found anything better than Lightroom and Premier Pro.

Canva — Unless you've got the skills and software of a graphic designer, you may need to come to grips with Canva. It enables someone with an eye, but without real skills, to create polished-looking designs. I use it most days to make pins for Pinterest and simple graphics for my blog.

VPN — While catching up on your favorite Netflix or HBO show might not be a priority, you'll find that you can't access some programming and platforms in certain parts of the world. Enabling a VPN on your laptop, phone, or tablet can also grant you access to some websites that are blocked in certain countries.

Splitwise — Even solo travelers need to split a complicated tab every now and then. Sometimes, you'll find yourself on a trip with your new travel buddies, and you paid up front for the accommodations, one person covered the train tickets, another friend picked up the check for breakfast, and another friend says she'll pay you all back next week. The Splitwise mobile app makes it easy to keep track of who paid for what and who owes what, even in multiple currencies.

TripIt — This mobile app stores confirmation information for your trips. When you buy a plane ticket, reserve a seat on a train, book an Airbnb or hotel stay, book a tour, or get tickets to an event, you simply forward the confirmation email to TripIt.

Chapter 18 - It's Okay To Go Home

Fun fact: You cannot fail at being a digital nomad.

The only failure is thinking that this lifestyle might be right for you, but never really going for it.

If you become a digital nomad only to discover three months later that this isn't the life you want — well, that is not failing. That's you making a choice, having a life experience, then making another choice. You will not regret trying--even if you realize it's not the life for you-- because you'll learn so much in the process.

You will, however, regret never having the guts to try.

In the past three years, I have gone 'home' several times. I returned home for weddings, to see family, and just to regroup and recharge. It did me a lot of good, emotionally, to take those trips home. Plus, I got to dump some of the useless things I packed the first time I left, and I was able to buy some much-needed gear.

If you're on the road and feeling burned out, homesick, and/or physically ill and exhausted, you should prioritize your health. Go home! Even when you're 'home', you're still a digital nomad. You can work wherever your computer is. So, take your computer and your sad ass, and fly home to family or friends for a bit. Sleep on their couch, if you have to, and soak up and dish out the love.

Then, when you're feeling recharged, you might feel that travel itch creeping up on you again. And you'll know it's time to hit the road…or not. There's no right or wrong way to live this life.

Chapter 17 - When Things Go Wrong

So, here's the thing. There is going to come a time when everything goes tits up. You're going to seriously question your life choices. If things go really wrong, you may find yourself looking for a one-way flight home.

Of course, life has its ups and downs. But when you're traveling on your own, those ups and downs can feel more intense. If you take my advice, when things go wrong you will already have your mental health plan in place. That's going to help a lot. But most of the time, you're just riding the wave and holding on for dear life.

I'd like to share two stories of times when things went seriously wrong.

The Scorpion Incident

I had no idea there are scorpions in Guatemala.

Had I known this particular fact and how partial they are to bamboo buildings, I may have questioned my choice of hostel. But I didn't find out until I was stung by a scorpion THREE times while I was sleeping.

Now, most people have a topical reaction to a scorpion sting similar to that of a bee sting. It swells up and hurts like hell. I, however, did not have a typical reaction. I had a full-blown neurological reaction. In short, I was unable to control my body and pretty much paralyzed for 12 hours. It was a full 24 hours before I was able to walk properly.

But that's not the worst of it. The worst thing was I was in a very remote area, alone (although there were some strangers asleep in the dorm), and I knew there was absolutely no way I would be able to get any medical help until the next day. So, I had to resign myself to the fact that I was going to either live or die, and there was nothing at all I could do about it other than try to stay awake, so I didn't slip away in my sleep.

It was terrifying.

But I kept myself calm and waited for morning before raising the alarm and getting someone to locate a doctor for me (because I'm British and it is embedded in my DNA never to cause a fuss unless you are 100% positive you are actually going to die). This is the reason I now never leave home without activated charcoal and antihistamine. I also splash tea tree oil around my bed before I sleep, and I always check for scorpions, no matter where I am in the world!

I'm not sharing this with you in an attempt to scare you. I'm telling you this story because I learned a lot about myself through the entire experience. I learned how mentally tough I had become. In the dark of the night, when I didn't know if I was going to see the next day, I felt calm. I knew I had lived my best life. I was right where I wanted to be, with no regrets.

I tried to hang on to that thought when this happened…

Broke and Robbed in Bogota

I didn't want to leave Guatemala. I had such a lovely life there. I was teaching yoga and meditation every day. I had free accommodations in exchange for managing a company's social media, and I had great friends. But, I knew it was time to go. Plus, I had an amazing job waiting for me in Bogota.

Oh, Colombia. This place broke me down and built me back up.

I booked an Airbnb with good reviews for three months in La Candelaria and got on the plane. Unfortunately, I hadn't been working much over the months before due to my mum getting married, a family vacation in Hawaii, and my yoga teacher training course. So, I arrived in Colombia with $50 in my pocket and nothing in my bank account. I'd paid my first month's rent, but that was it. I was flat broke in a new city where I knew no one, and for the first time, I was living on my own, not in a hostel. I had a job choreographing for a dance company, but it offered just two hours a week.

This lifestyle is never going to be easy, but I honestly didn't expect it to get quite this bad.

I'm not going to detail the miserable two months I spent there, but I'll admit that my problem was my lack of cash. A client owed me $600, but their payment went "missing." This left me in a complete mess, and I had to borrow money from my parents. I needed to get my finances back under control and have a steady paycheck. So, this experience led me to teach English online, which was actually a super smart move. By the time I left Colombia the following year, I was in a solid financial position.

But Bogota was cold, gray, polluted, and dangerous. And I was broke. I spent most of my time in my damp apartment, wishing I'd never left Guatemala. Even when I had some money, the thought of having to go to a shop and ask for things with my terrible Spanish made me want to cry.

My apartment was in a dangerous area, and I lived opposite drug dealers. This meant there were always people in the street buying drugs. All of my friends lived in the north of the city, so I never went out at night because I couldn't get home safely.

In addition to teaching English online, I started teaching English at a local school. I taught 121 classes, mostly for teenagers, to help them prep for exams. This was a lot of work and required me to travel all over the city to teach, but it didn't pay well. My boss was a bit of a nightmare and didn't pay me on time, so I had to go on strike to get paid.

Then, just to top things off, my phone was stolen. This broke me.

Yes, it was just a phone. But when you feel as low and as lonely as I did then, your phone is a lifeline. And I couldn't afford to buy a new one. At this point, I had lived in Bogota for two months. My choreography job was coming to an end, and I'd already decided I wasn't going to teach for the local school anymore. The only thing keeping me in that city was the commitment I'd made to my landlady. I told her I would stay for an extra month.

As I cried myself to sleep, I suddenly had this realization. I'm a digital nomad. I don't have to stay here. I don't have to stay anywhere. So, I posted in the Digital Nomad Colombia Facebook group asking for suggestions, and everyone told me to go to Medellín. I booked a flight the next day and broke the news to my landlady. She was a bit annoyed but, quite frankly, I was past caring.

When I arrived in Medellín, it was like the sun had come out again. I found an amazing place to stay the next day with awesome roomies. I had an incredible few months living there.

So please remember, when things don't work out, move on!

P.S. Don't let my story turn you off from going to Bogota. I'd honestly go back in a heartbeat—just with better, safer accommodations. If you want recommendations about Colombia, check my blog or drop me an email.

Chapter 19 - Conclusion

This is the point where I'm supposed to deliver a profound and inspiring conclusion. But you've already learned the many reasons why I chose and continue to choose the digital nomad lifestyle. You know why I prefer to travel by myself. And hopefully you've come to terms with the truth that being a DN doesn't always look and feel like it does on social media. The reality is, it's something so much greater, but far less glamourous and predictable.

Being a digital nomad is not the life for everyone, and it may not be something you want to do forever. But I hope you now have a clearer and more realistic idea of what it's like to make the transition to digital nomadism and what it's like to live out in the world as a solo female full-time traveler.

If you're still thinking this life may be for you, you're better equipped now to take the plunge. You've got my personal travel stories to keep in mind and some practical rules and tools to put this idea of yours into action.

Every decision you make is a step toward the unknown. Some of your decisions feel more secure than other. This one might be risky, but what is life without risk?

About the Author

Claire Summers is a dedicated traveler and Digital Nomad. At 34 she sold all her worldly possessions that wouldn't fit into 3 boxes or in her backpack and hit the road. She travels slowly and with purpose to places many think women shouldn't go alone. She has lived in Guatemala, Colombia, and Mexico while traveling extensively in Latin America.

Through her blog and books Claire wants to inspire other women to travel more with less fear. You can visit her blog www.clairesitchyfeet.com to follow along with her travels.

www.ingramcontent.com/pod-product-compliance
Lightning Source LLC
Chambersburg PA
CBHW030657220526
45463CB00005B/1813